A **child** MAGAZINE GUIDE

FEELING SAFE
Talking to Children
About War and Terrorism

0760746818

A **child** MAGAZINE GUIDE

FEELING SAFE
Talking to Children
About War and Terrorism

FROM THE EDITORS OF CHILD MAGAZINE

BARNES
&NOBLE
BOOKS
NEW YORK

Library of Congress Cataloging-in-Publication Data Available upon request

Feeling Safe: Talking to Children About War and Terrorism

ISBN: 0760746818

Printed and bound in the United States of America

03 04 05 06 07 MP 9 8 7 6 5 4 3 2 1

Contents

Contents

Part Two:
Learning From Others   45

Introduction

Parenthood is challenging under the best of circumstances. At a time when we're all surrounded by constant talk and images of war and terrorism, mothers and fathers are faced with even greater questions and concerns. Sometimes children express their confusion, fears, and anxieties directly and ask the tough questions. In other cases they don't let on that they're worried about anything, and it's not until later that we discover they've been plagued by underlying doubts and tensions.

But none of us—no matter what the age of our children or how they seem to be responding to the world situation—can put our heads in the sand and pretend that there aren't grave issues that must be addressed. What parents and early childhood educators discovered after the horrific events on September 11, 2001, was that even very young children understood, on some level, that a colossal tragedy had occurred. All over the country, mothers, fathers, childcare providers, and preschool teachers reported with amazement that toddlers and preschoolers were building towers from toy blocks and then crashing them down...over and over and over again. The images these young ones had seen on television, the adult conversations they'd overheard, and the snippets of information they'd picked up from friends at daycare, preschool, or kindergarten all had their impact.

It's important to be prepared to answer our kids' questions when they arise (and they usually do at the most inopportune moments!), but it is probably even more essential to be proactive. While we can't guarantee children a safe world, we can reassure them, provide them with a feeling of being safe, and as they grow older, arm them with the greater sophistication and knowledge they'll need to understand world events. Parenthood challenges us to be the best we can be, and it's times like these—when we have to offer our children stability and reassurance in the face of danger and talk of violence—that truly test our mettle.

At *Child* magazine our mission is to provide our readers with inspiration and the best information possible. We're so fortunate to have access to the greatest thinkers about parenthood and childhood today. I'd like to thank all the experts who contributed their insights to the pages that follow. The members of *Child*'s illustrious advisory board have been, as they always are, extremely generous and helpful in sharing their perspectives. I'm also very lucky to have a staff of editors at *Child* who are thoroughly committed to the role our magazine plays in presenting parents with the essential guidance they need to raise their children well. I want to thank Kara Corridan, senior editor at *Child*, for spearheading this book with such dedication; Andrea Barbalich, *Child*'s executive editor, for reading and finessing every word; Kathy Henderson, our lifestyle director, for her superb editing and writing skills; Robert Kelly for his impeccable attention to detail in copyediting; Maureen Ryan for her thorough fact-checking; Dan Josephs for his art suggestions; and Jennifer Bush, Polly Chevalier, Carmela Ciuraru, Lindsey Crittenden, Emily Fromm, Lisa Frydman, Laura Gilbert, Gershom Gorenberg, Rory Halperin, Jane Hammerslough, Pamela Kruger, Sandra Lee, Topaz Le Tourneau, Tracy Perez, and Pamela Vu for their hard work and invaluable contributions. Thank you to Laura Nolan, senior editor at Barnes & Noble Publishing, for recognizing the importance of such a book, creative director Jeff Batzli and art director Kevin Ullrich, and the rest of the Barnes & Noble Publishing staff for their enthusiasm and support.

Finally, I want to share a story an older friend of mine recently related to me. She is a woman now in her sixties, originally from Montreal, and she recalls a train journey she took with her parents during a frigid Canadian winter when she was a young child. The train broke down in the middle of the night and sat, without heat or electricity, for four hours. My friend recalls feeling indescribably cold and fearful of the dark. Yet as her father sat with her, holding her closely for warmth and reassuring her in his calm and loving manner, she began to feel safe and relaxed. She notes that the nurturing, comforting, caring support her dad provided that night has been a gift for a lifetime. He offered her the feeling of being cherished and safe—and the sense that all was ultimately right with the world. She maintains that such reassurance has gotten her through many difficult times in adulthood.

And so I wish for all of you, for all of us, as parents, an ability to provide our children with a safety blanket. I hope that the guidance we offer in the pages that follow will help you give your children the smart, reassuring answers they need and the nurturing and love that are so vital to helping them thrive.

Miriam Arond
Editor in Chief
Child Magazine

Part One

—

The Right Words

—

To help you begin your conversations with children about issues
as confusing and upsetting as violence, war, and terrorism, we've
gone straight to those who know how to do it best. We've con-
sulted child psychiatrists and psychologists—many of whom have
counseled families in the aftermath of September 11—for their
suggestions on the most effective and least frightening ways to
broach these subjects. Equally important, these experts provide
age-specific advice so you'll understand exactly when children
can grasp the complexities surrounding topics such as anti-
Americanism and bioterrorism. In addition, we've asked parents
across the United States to share what they're telling their children.
This section also contains advice geared toward those children
who have loved ones in the military and for whom world events
take on a much more personal meaning. In the final chapter
we address how to head off a potential byproduct of the crisis:
children's prejudice toward other cultures.

"What Is War?"

—

Starting the conversation

—

By Andrea Barbalich

"It's hard enough for me to understand what's going on in the world, much less figure out what to say to my child." This sentiment, so common among parents today, expresses the confusion and bewilderment that go along with life in the early 21st century. And it's true—it *is* difficult to know what to say to children when so much in our lives seems so very different from how it was a few short years ago.

Still, it's important to find a way. Children count on adults to help them make sense of confusing events and feel safe when those events seem frightening. For an overview of how to handle a sensitive responsibility, we turned to Erik Kolbell, a psychotherapist and ordained minister in New York City who specializes in family therapy. He counseled families during the Gulf War in 1991 and after the September 11 terrorist attacks. He is also the author of *Lifescripts for Family and Friends*, a book about having conversations on difficult topics with people you care about.

How can you explain concepts as complex as war and terrorism to a child?

You can't fool children, especially today, because of the immediacy of war. Journalists are there on the battlefield covering conflicts as they're happening, the news is reported around the clock, and adults are talking about it constantly. Everything is right in front of kids. So you can't lie to them, and you really can't cover up the ugliness of war. What you can do is find ways to answer their questions calmly and simply. This helps assure them that, especially during difficult times, the adults around them are doing everything possible to protect them.

What kinds of questions do children typically ask?

Is this happening here? How far away is it? Do we know anybody who's fighting? Are the people we're fighting against going to be looking for me or my family? Are children dying? Why are we fighting? In every case, you want to be truthful with your children without giving more details than they can handle.

What do you recommend saying to a child who asks, "What is a war?"

First, I would give some background. I would say that problems or conflicts are not inherently bad—conflicts are just conflicts. They happen. The question is how you work those conflicts out. I would then go on to say that war is often an expression of the inability of two countries to work out their differences in a peaceable manner. And in that way, there's a lesson for kids on how to respond to disagreements in their own life.

War can be instructive. It provides an opportunity to talk about how we can resolve conflicts without hurting people.

I have also found that when kids are faced with images of war, it's helpful to generate a discussion about what they can do for people who face difficulties on a smaller scale. If you ask children for suggestions, they come up with tangible things. They may say, for example, "If my friend is sick and misses school, I can call her up and see if she needs anything." If another child is feeling pain about something, your child might go over and ask, "Can I sit with you at lunch today?" If another child's favorite toy is broken, your child may say, "That happened to me too" or "Would you like to share mine?" These things create a certain camaraderie among the children, and someday they'll understand that this kind of connection is an antidote to what gives rise to war. The more you feel in common with someone, the less likely you are to want to do battle with that person.

At what age should you start discussing world events with children?

It depends on the child and the child's exposure to the media. If you keep a child under 3 away from the news reports and watch what you say in front of her, she'll probably have no idea that anything unpleasant is happening—and that's fine.

Kids ages 3 to 5 may have some idea, and for that age group the important thing is instilling in them a sense of security: "Countries are fighting far away from here. They are trying to end it as quickly as possible. In the meantime we will do everything in the world to protect you." As a way to help understand

what your child is processing—and may not be able to verbalize—
you might provide opportunities for her to express herself through
play. Ask her to draw or use blocks or other creative toys to share
her feelings.

A 5- or 6-year-old who is involved with other kids and
watches television and knows what's going on may have her
antennae up, but she's too young to understand why it's happening. You want to give the same general reassurances, and you
also want to explain that this is not a video game. There are many
caricatures of war in entertainment that can become the child's
definition of war.

At ages 7 and 8, you want to talk to your children more
openly, saying, "This is a real thing. This is not make-believe.
None of the countries involved are happy about it. They have
failed to resolve their conflict in a peaceful way. They tried and
they failed." Then ask questions to open a dialogue with your
kids. They will feel more empowered if you're really engaging
them in discussion. "How would you solve it? How would you
work it out with your friends?" Smoke out any hidden fears,
such as fears of being alone and being separated from parents,
and any instances where kids' imagination might be running
away from them.

For older children, ages 9 and up, you can be a little more
specific: "Two countries decided that this is what they need
to do to protect their citizens. This is a method of last resort.
Eventually what happens is that the fighting stops. And when
that happens, the goal is to have some kind of agreement where
all citizens will feel protected."

Teenagers have their own opinions. So you can do more asking and engage them on a basic political level: "These are the roots of this conflict as I understand them. What's your opinion? What would you do if you were the leader of America or the United Nations? What do you think of war?"

You can also discuss with kids, from about age 7 onward, what they are going to encounter that is out of the ordinary: "You'll be seeing more police officers. The airports are different. These are signs that our government is doing even more to protect us." There's no denying that life is different for our kids now than it was before. Try to help them find some comfort and assurance in it.

How much should parents try to limit children's exposure to the war and other frightening events?

Visuals, especially moving pictures, are inherently seductive. I would not only be vigilant about what my child is seeing, but I would actually legislate it: "Here's how much TV is going to go on in this house. Here's what's off limits." In general, the less young children see and read about what's going on, the better. For very young children, I would keep the TV off altogether.

War, of course, isn't the only thing that's on people's minds right now. How can you explain the concept of terrorism to a child?

You want to find a way to say that people can have beliefs that are deeply felt but also tremendously misguided. This depends heavily on the age of the child, but do your best to explain how, when people are different and differences come into conflict, conflicts can grow. If people can't find a way to work out the problem, it gets worse and worse and sometimes gets out of control, and that's when it gives rise to such drastic behavior. As always, try to find some kind of parallel to the child's life. Kids can understand humiliation and frustration and the sense of anger that grows with humiliation.

At some point, though, don't you need to tell the child that terrorism is wrong?

Parents have to decide what kind of ethical lessons they're trying to teach their children. They should pinpoint them and then say, "These are the things our family believes." Some of these things could be: It's always wrong to take a life. It's wrong for someone who's strong to exercise that strength over someone who's weak. It's wrong for someone who's rich to take advantage of someone who's poor. Decide what you want your child to believe is unacceptable behavior, and then say, "These are all things our family doesn't approve of."

In children's minds, and even in some adults', this can eventually boil down to an issue of good people vs. bad people. If a child speaks in those terms, how should you respond?

It's very easy to see the world as black and white, as good against evil. In that kind of world the rules are simple: We're on the side of good, and anyone who isn't is on the side of evil. But that line of reasoning doesn't take into consideration the ambiguities that are very much a part of life. Few things are ever really that simple.

So my advice would be to steer children away from thinking about good guys and bad guys. Children need to come to an understanding that good people sometimes do things that aren't good and that all of us can be driven to do things we're not happy about. It's better to speak in terms of people's behavior—to talk about the bad things someone has done, rather than say the person is bad. Otherwise, it's easy for children to overlook the fact that those we're fighting against are flesh and blood human beings.

Should parents reveal their own fear, worry, sadness, and other emotions to their kids?

Young children do not want to believe in parents' vulnerability. Their parents' job is to protect them. If parents of young kids have emotional things to say about the war or other world events, I would advise doing it out of earshot. And if your child comes to you with questions, try to answer them calmly and rationally, without getting upset.

For kids who are a little older, preteens and up, it's okay to let some of your feelings show. You can say, "This thing really has me rattled. I'm concerned about this war, so I'm going to write the President." Or "I'm thinking about the troops, so I'm going to write letters to the soldiers." If you are a family of active religious belief, you can say you're going to take your feelings to your god. You can also drive the point home: "This is bothering me, so I'm going to leave work earlier because I want to be with you guys." That conveys the humanity of the parent and also sends a message about the importance of coping with the situation in a constructive way. And of course, you can involve kids in whatever active steps you decide to take: They can help write letters to the troops, send donations to the Red Cross, invite a child whose mom or dad is fighting in the war over to play, and so forth.

How should parents answer a child's questions when they don't know the answers themselves?

You can say, "We don't know right now, but we might know more tomorrow or we might know more next week."

What is the most important piece of advice you would give to a parent during these trying times?

Let your kids know at every opportunity that they're looked after and they're loved, that your family is strong and cohesive and enduring.

2

The Politics of War

—

Explaining challenging concepts to children

—

By Carmela Ciuraru

During times of political turmoil, even well-informed adults can find it difficult to articulate their feelings about America's role in world affairs. Imagine how confusing the politics of war and terrorism are for kids, especially when images of brave soldiers are juxtaposed with angry protests and words of condemnation from other countries.

"Children can't sort out the subtleties and logic that went into our government's decision to go to war—their thinking is much more simple and concrete," says Diane Levin, Ph.D., professor of education at Wheelock College in Boston, Massachusetts, author of six books, including *Teaching Young Children in Violent Times*, and an expert on how to counteract the effects of violence and media culture on children. "A lot of kids are confused because we tell them to 'use your words' to solve conflicts and not to fight. Suddenly they see grown-ups fighting, and that's a scary thing; it's like the world is topsy-turvy. Saying, 'Sometimes you just have to fight,' doesn't help them deal adequately with that confusion."

When kids begin asking questions about war, experts agree that you should consider their level of maturity first—and then proceed slowly. "The most important thing a parent can do is to really listen to what kids say and not make any assumptions about what they're thinking, what worries them, or what they're afraid of," says Buffy Smith, Ph.D., staff psychologist at the Bank Street School for Children in New York City. "It's not in the best interest of kids to give them big lectures on the principles of war. Instead, as much as you can, get a sense of what they're concerned about, and respond in ways that address their questions. Put out a little bit of information, and see what their next question is. Read their body language and see if they're turning off or being overloaded."

Regardless of your personal political views, it's helpful to read how Drs. Levin and Smith advise dealing with a trio of potentially sticky questions.

"Why did we go to war?"

For children younger than 8, most questions concerning the reasons for war are actually tied to fears about personal safety. "Young children relate everything to themselves," Dr. Levin says. "Taking different points of view into account is difficult for them. When they see or hear something, they think, 'How will this affect me? Will I be hurt?' That egocentrism is normal. So the first step is always to ask children what they know and what they've heard. You want to figure out what they're really asking before you explain anything."

Agrees Dr. Smith, "It's tricky to try to answer young children's questions because they're cognitively not ready to understand the nuances of war. Parents often want to explain the complexities of the situation and help them empathize with the lives of children in other countries, but a very young child can't get beyond a simplistic view of things." The task is to reinforce the idea that you will do everything you can to keep your kids safe.

School-age children can handle a basic discussion about the reasons for war and the varying viewpoints people hold—and they often ask surprisingly complex questions. "I just heard about a third-grader who asked, 'If Saddam Hussein is so bad, how did he get to be president of his country?'" says Dr. Levin. "Another child asked, 'If Saddam Hussein is so bad, why did God make him?'" These kinds of questions call for a more thoughtful and complete response.

Try to be clear about the different views people have, explaining that America's leaders believed war was the only way to bring freedom to Iraq and to remove a dangerous man from power. Other people feel that President Bush could have worked harder to find other ways to stop Saddam Hussein so there didn't have to be a war. "Just give a little piece of information," emphasizes Dr. Levin, "and let your child respond. When you finish, you can say, 'I'm glad you asked me about this, and we can talk about it again, if you want to.'"

If you keep the conversation neutral, children can start to develop skills in critical thinking and an ability to look at world events through a broader lens—understanding, for example, that it's possible to support our troops while still being against the war those troops are fighting. Says Dr. Levin, "Whatever you think about recent conflicts, our goal is to raise children who don't see war as the first resort when there is a problem between countries."

"Why do people protest war?"

When children see war-related rallies on television, the images can seem violent; often the protesters appear angry. Again, the initial goal is to reassure kids that they are safe. Then, depending on the child's age, you can explain that the protesters don't want to hurt anyone; they simply have different views about the war and are gathering to express how they feel and send a message to our leaders. This conversation should be quite positive: "We are so fortunate in America to have the freedom to say exactly how we feel about issues, even if we disagree with the President."

Dr. Levin recalls bringing her son to protest rallies when he was as young as 5 because, for younger children, witnessing a concrete event is helpful. Dr. Smith, however, cautions parents who might consider involving young children in political marches. "Seeing angry faces and hearing angry voices can be a scary thing for a 4- or 5-year-old at a rally," she says. "Kids can easily misinterpret what's going on." As children approach adolescence, though, expressing their emerging views can be a positive experience. "Taking part in a rally can give some kids a sense that their opinion is valued and they're part of something bigger than themselves," Dr. Smith says. "It can actually reinforce family values."

"Why do other countries seem to hate us?"

Children who remember the outpouring of sympathy our country received after September 11 will no doubt be confused by anti-American sentiment. The first response is the simplest: Countries don't always agree. As with the other questions, it's valuable for kids to know that other political views are worthy of consideration.

"As kids get older, they are increasingly able to handle complex and even negative information," says Dr. Smith, who has observed lively discussions of world politics at her school. "The whole idea of patriotism, who's good and who's bad, and why people in other countries don't like us—these are interesting issues to explore." For kids too young to join the debate, it's enough to emphasize that differences are okay.

"I advise parents to help kids understand that there are all kinds of viewpoints. And if they can take in as many as possible they won't grow up thinking in terms of stereotypes: black, white, good, bad," says Dr. Levin. "Society is enriched by difference. That idea needs to be reinforced," adds Dr. Smith.

If you find yourself feeling disconcerted by world events, Dr. Smith urges honesty and simplicity. "When your child expresses confusion about anti-Americanism or other things in the news, he's giving you the opportunity to have an empathetic moment," she says. "My first response would be, 'You and me both! This is a confusing time.' And I'd go from there, taking my lead from the child and letting him know that I appreciate the fact that these subjects are overwhelming. Nobody can unravel the whole thing, but parents can try to understand a child's feelings—and maybe, with that small step, begin to feel better."

3

How Parents Reassure Their Children

—

Stories from families across the country

—

Compiled by Rory Halperin

At dinner tables across the United States, mealtime chatter that was once based on homework, sports updates, and weekend plans has turned to discussions of war, violence, and death. As you well know, children are bringing up concerns you've probably never had to think about addressing. We at *Child* asked our readers to share what their kids have been asking and what they're saying in response. Even though many of them had differing opinions of world events, there's one thing they all agreed on: Making sure their children feel safe, comfortable, loved, and protected is a priority. Read on as parents nationwide relate the words and actions that have helped comfort and reassure their own children.

"I made sure to advise my 6-year-old daughter, Erica, about what was happening before she received distorted information from friends at school. The night the war in Iraq broke out, I explained that there are men who pose a threat to our country and our President and others have decided that we need to stop them before they hurt any more people. We've discussed that the war is being fought far away and that our soldiers are doing everything in their power to keep us safe. We make sure to say a prayer for the men and women fighting for our safety, for their families, and for the innocent people living in Iraq."

Danalynn Sattler
Selden, New York

"'Is this show still on?' in reference to the war coverage and 'Is this really happening, or is it a movie?' are two of the questions my 5-year-old daughter, Riley, has asked. I tell her that yes, it's real, but she shouldn't worry because the fighting is taking place far from our home. We also talk about the soldiers she sees on television and how they have families at home who miss them very much. It makes her feel better to know that the soldiers can communicate with their loved ones via e-mail. We've also been spending a lot more time outside gardening, riding bikes, and playing soccer. I want the kids to have other things to focus on."

Georgia Sanchez
Austin, Texas

"Although my 10-month-old daughter and 3-year-old son are too young to really understand the war in Iraq, I feel that it's my responsibility to make sure they feel as safe and secure as possible in their own little world. I keep up a daily routine, such as family dinnertime and walks to the neighborhood park, and involve them in activities that teach valuable lessons. We just enrolled my son in his first organized sport, T-ball, in which he'll learn about being on a team and working with others. I find it touching that these concepts also apply to the lives of our American soldiers who depend upon one another on the battlefield."

Constance Margarite Briggs
Acworth, Georgia

"Since we live in New York City, my 9-year-old daughter, Nicole, is extremely concerned about how the war will affect our safety at home. Some days she asks lots of questions; other days she doesn't want to hear or talk about the war. She says it makes her sick to her stomach. She's asked, 'Will I live to be 10?' and 'Is Saddam Hussein going to blow us up?' How do I answer questions like these? I have been telling her that our President and government are doing all they can to keep us safe. I keep my 4-year-old and 14-month-old completely away from the war coverage on television, but from time to time, Nicole asks to watch the news. I make sure to watch with her so I can discuss issues and answer questions that may arise."

Lorraine DeGorter
Brooklyn, New York

"Even though she's only 5, my daughter is extremely aware of and interested in world events. She sat with us and watched as the President told the nation we were going to war. Using words that she can understand, I explained that the president wants to make sure that the people who have harmed our country are stopped. I've showed her where Iraq is on a map, so she knows just how far away we are from the fighting."

Rosita Thomas
Manassas, Virginia

"Both my 4- and 7-year-old daughters have been asking if we are trying to kill the bad guys. My older girl is extremely concerned with the 'regular people standing around,' the civilians, while my younger is very matter-of-fact when she speaks of the war. She'll say, 'The United States is trying to kill that man, and the bad people are trying to kill us.' When these questions and comments arise, we discuss what war is and how people may die during a war. They've asked if they could pray for those who are fighting, so now we've started praying for the war to end quickly. Although their viewing of war coverage on television is kept to a minimum, they do hear a lot at school. I make sure to discuss these events with them daily to clear up any confusion they have."

Veronica Kelley
Orange County, California

"We did most of the talking about war before my 4-year-old son's godfather, a United States Marine, left for Afghanistan a number of months ago. From time to time, I'll find him and my 8-year-old son playing war and replaying the September 11 attacks. I take these opportunities to jump into their play and discuss the issues with them. I also make sure that our entire family is doing something to support the troops. We write letters and send pictures to the Marines and hang yellow ribbons outside our home."

D. Ann Turoczy
Wescosville, Pennsylvania

"Our six children—who range in age from 3 to 12—are extremely concerned about the children living in Iraq. At one of our family meetings, my 6-year-old asked, 'Do the kids sit in their houses all day waiting for the bombs to stop?' while my 9-year-old wondered if the children still attended school. I honestly wasn't sure how to answer these questions, but I tried to explain that most Iraqi families had fled their cities when they knew the war was inevitable. To help reassure our children that kids just like them more than a world away were okay, we decided to start a letter-writing campaign between American and Iraqi schoolchildren."

Ginny Bishop
Littleton, Colorado

"When we found out my husband was being called for duty, we sat my 6-year-old daughter down and told her that Daddy had to leave for a while to help find the people who had done bad things. Of course, her first question was, 'When will he come back?' Now that he's overseas, I'm very clear with Emily as to what's going on. We talk about the soldiers and how, unfortunately, sometimes accidents happen that prevent them from coming home to their families. Emily has made some comments about how she hates the bad people. I try to teach her that we don't hate anyone. I've also put pictures of Daddy at eye level on the fridge so Emily and her 2½-year-old sister can feel closer to their father."

Debbie Jones
Flowery Brand, Georgia

 *4*

When a Loved One Answers the Call to Duty

—

Comforting children with family and friends in the military

—

By Pamela Vu

For many children, war and terrorism hit very close to home. Roughly 1.2 million kids have parents actively serving in the military, and 600,000 more have mothers and fathers in the National Guard and Reserve, according to the Military Family Resource Center in Arlington, Virginia. There's no way to quantify how many kids have family friends, neighbors, and other relatives in the armed forces. But what's certain is that all these children face burdens most of their peers don't. They must deal with separation anxiety and limited information about where their loved ones are, when they'll return, and whether they're safe.

Though children with family and friends in the military may experience heightened anxiety or fear, parents, other relatives, caregivers, and friends can play a crucial role in minimizing those reactions and helping kids cope and thrive, says Stephen J. Cozza,

M.D., chief of the department of psychiatry at the Walter Reed Army Medical Center in Washington, DC. Adults can discuss their feelings and find support among peers, but children, especially young ones, may have a tougher time. What follows is a breakdown of the ways kids of all ages react when their loved one is deployed and the best ways to help them.

Ages 2 and under Babies and toddlers won't understand why a parent or caregiver is leaving, but they can sense that the people around them are worried or withdrawn. "A lot of the reactions of young children who can't yet talk depend on the reactions of people close to them," says Dr. Cozza, who has counseled children in military families for more than 15 years. Indeed, scores of studies—including recent research from the Traumatic Stress Studies Program at Mount Sinai School of Medicine in New York City—illustrate that in anxious times, children and adolescents respond to adults' feelings and reactions.

Ages 3 to 5 Preschoolers worry primarily about their own safety when a parent is away. Their new family arrangement may be confusing and distressing to them. By maintaining morning and bedtime rituals and continuing family traditions such as movie night or visits to Grandma's house, kids will regain a sense of security and control over their world. Staying in touch with a deployed loved one through letters, cards, photographs, or kids' artwork helps comfort children and keep them feeling connected.

Kids this age may also believe it's their fault that a person is leaving ("I got angry with Daddy, and that's why he left"). In that case, explain to your child that it's Daddy's job to serve in the military to help her understand that her father is not abandoning her because of something she said or did. Some children may even be angry with a parent for leaving. Others may experience sleep disturbances, loss of appetite, bedwetting, fear of the dark, and other regressive behaviors. They may be clingy with their parent or caregiver and prefer the company of adults to children their own age.

Ages 6 to 12 By the time kids are in elementary school, they'll pick up information from the television, radio, or Internet. "It's vital to ask them about their fears, emotions, and thoughts," says Dr. Cozza. They're also more likely to ask specific questions, perhaps wondering when their older cousin is coming home from the war, how far the United States is from the fighting, and even about death. If your 6-year-old asks, "Will Uncle Joe be killed?" you can respond with a question of your own: "Is that something you've been worried about?" It's also healthy for children to know how you're feeling. You can say, "I'm worried about Uncle Joe, too, but the servicemen and women are taking very good care of him while he's there. He's very good at his job and he feels confident about what he's doing. But it's scary for us because if we had to do his job, we wouldn't know how."

Ages 13 to 18 Teenagers will be able to understand broader issues of war, its indefinite nature, and the lack of information about a loved one ("We're not sure where Daddy is"). But the stress of an absent parent or authority figure, on top of the typical turmoil of adolescence, can surface as inappropriate sexual behavior, a decline in school performance, depression, or drug and alcohol abuse. Teens know how to hide their feelings but need reassurances as well. Maintain rules in the home and be consistent in disciplining kids this age. Volunteering in the community, helping with household chores, or tutoring a younger child are some ways to help teens focus on something positive that can help lessen their feelings of helplessness and anxiety.

It's understandable for families with loved ones in the armed services to spend more time watching television news coverage of war-related events than other households. But parents need to be mindful of their children's reaction to the information. Parents should not leave their preschooler or school-age child to watch TV alone. These children have a hard time separating fact from fantasy. "If they see an injured soldier on the screen, for example, they may believe that everyone who goes into the military will meet this fate," explains Dr. Cozza. Tell your child that this is one picture of just one person who is hurt and that there are doctors and nurses who will help him get better. "This reassures the child of her family member's safety and provides her with an explanation about what's happening," he says. Of course, it's also helpful to turn off the TV to give kids a chance to put their worries aside.

Obviously, deployment leads to increased stress for the remaining parent, who must deal with all the family responsibilities while trying to manage her own fears and sadness. If Mom is unable to provide the same level of attention, care, and nurturing she could before deployment, she should ask relatives and friends for help. Perhaps someone can cook a meal once a week, babysit for a few hours, or do laundry. A neighbor might take a child to the pool, on a bike ride, or out to a baseball game. "Parents need to realize that they can be the best advocates for their children only if they're mentally and physically healthy," says Dr. Cozza. "Even if your school has a counseling program that addresses how to cope, it won't do your child any good if she comes home to a depressed parent who spent the day in bed." There are also many resources available through the military system, including family assistance centers, chaplains, and wives' clubs. "It's important that families seek out assistance when they feel the need," he says.

It's also important to remind children that it's all right to be a kid and to have fun during this stressful time. Playing sports, going to the park, or taking a day trip are all healthy distractions. The goal, says Dr. Cozza, is to support children so they continue to grow and develop in the absence of their deployed parent.

If your child is having difficulties adjusting, seek professional help from a pediatrician or a mental health provider, preferably one who works closely with children and adolescents. Schools that serve a significant number of children from military families may already have programs in place to help kids deal with deployment. Teachers, principals, and school counselors can also be wonderful resources. Their day-to-day interaction with kids allows them to pick up on signs of anxiety.

For certain children the loss may be felt more acutely. Those with existing emotional, behavioral, or developmental problems may be more vulnerable and fragile in this situation. Deployment of a single parent is especially hard on a child who may have to stay with relatives in a new home. In such a case parents should give alternative childcare arrangements careful thought and discuss them in advance to help prepare their child.

If a parent has not been called to serve yet but is expected to, it's best to tell children 7 and older right away, says Dr. Cozza. Younger kids, however, don't benefit from advance notice—they may end up obsessing over the pending separation. One month's warning is probably sufficient. Ultimately, it's up to parents to decide when is the right time to notify their child. The key is to have time for these discussions so that everyone in the family is reassured and clear about the changes to come and so there's plenty of time to say goodbye. Also crucial to ensuring a healthy response from a child: sharing the news calmly and acknowledging the inevitable feelings it brings up—sadness, disappointment, and even anger, says Dr. Cozza.

Consider these additional suggestions offered by, among others, the American Academy of Child & Adolescent Psychiatry to help your child cope with separation.

- Encourage your child to express himself through creative outlets, such as drawing, coloring, building with blocks, and playing dress-up. Children who may not want to talk about their fears can often work out their feelings through play.

- Entrust your child with a responsibility. The task can be as simple as carrying place mats to the dinner table or putting away socks in drawers. This says to the child that he is a valued member of the family.

- Have reminders of the absent parent in the home. Display photographs and mementos, and record your spouse reading your child's favorite bedtime story and play it from time to time.

- Keep the deployed parent informed and involved in family activities. Help your child stay in touch by sending letters, e-mail messages, report cards, and school pictures.

- Involve your child's school, camp, and teachers. Let them know that your child's loved one is away, and ask them to be on the lookout for signs of vulnerability and stress.

5

Ready for Anything

—

Addressing safety measures with your child

—

By Kara Corridan

While it's important to know the right steps to take to prepare for possible emergencies, it's equally crucial to know how to do this in a way that doesn't scare children. Tempting as it may be to fill your child in on all the safety measures you're taking and to explain them in the broader context of war and terrorism, it's generally not advisable, says David Fassler, M.D., trustee of the American Psychiatric Association. "Procedures and explanations should be designed to help support and reassure children rather than further exacerbate a state of already heightened anxiety."

Remember that war and terrorist threats are just the latest stressors our children have faced. "We've been dealing with school violence, family violence, September 11, sniper shootings, anthrax fears, and the space shuttle disaster, along with the war in Iraq and the increased concerns about terrorism here," says Dr. Fassler, who is also clinical associate professor of psychiatry at the University of Vermont in Burlington. "All of this has had a cumulative effect on children."

When you broach the topic of preparing for emergencies, tailor your words depending on your child's age. For children under 8, a simple "These are good things to know to keep ourselves safe" should suffice. You can be more detailed with older children. Try something like: "A lot of people in this country are thinking about safety issues and they've come up with plans that seem pretty reasonable, so we think it makes sense to put them in place."

The following recommendations come from the American Red Cross and the Federal Emergency Management Agency (FEMA):

1. Find out your community's risks. Ask your local emergency management office or your American Red Cross chapter which disasters could strike your area. Are hazardous materials produced, stored, or transported near your town? Ask officials how to prepare for and respond to possible emergencies, as well as for any information that might reduce your risks.

2. Create an emergency communications plan. Help your child memorize his address, his phone number, and a number where he can reach each of his parents. For children as young as 4, you can turn the lesson into a project by using play dough and number-shaped cookie cutters to create these numerals.

Choose a relative or friend for you and your family to contact in the event that a crisis occurs and it's difficult to reach one another by phone. That person should then contact anyone else who needs to know your whereabouts. (And she should live far enough away from you that she'd be less likely to be involved in the same event.) All family members should have several ways to get in touch with the key person—including cell phone, fax, and e-mail—and let her know they're safe. It's smart to give your child's school and camp this information too.

3. Know your school's and camp's emergency plan. Will they keep your children there until a parent or designated adult picks them up, or will they be sent home on the bus? What kind of authorization do they need to release your child to an adult you've chosen? Do they have updated contact information for you?

4. Keep spare cash on hand. This way you're covered if the ATMs stop working.

5. Make sure your gas tank is full. If the power is out, gas pumps cannot work.

6. Assemble a disaster supply kit. You'll feel more at ease knowing that these items are in one place:

- three-day (or more) supply of water (one gallon per person per day) and nonperishable food

- can opener

- first-aid supplies

- prescription medication (make sure it hasn't expired)

- food and medication for family pets
- change of clothing and sleeping bag for each person in your home
- battery-powered radio or television
- flashlights
- batteries

Keep individual items in airtight plastic bags, and store everything in a duffel bag or an unused trash can. FEMA advises preparing three such kits: one for your home, one for your office, and one for your car. The car kit should also contain flares, jumper cables, and seasonal supplies like a shovel, ice scraper, and antifreeze.

Some experts feel it helps to involve children older than 10 in assembling these items because it offers a sense of control; others, such as Dr. Fassler, believe this might scare children and that it's enough to simply explain that your family has such a kit. Of course, the explanation will vary depending on their age. For a child under 5 who sees you stockpiling water and canned goods, for example, you might leave it at, "It never hurts for us to have extra water and food." But you may have to explain this a few times, since young children often find it reassuring to have things repeated, says Dr. Fassler. You can offer 6- to 10-year-olds an analogy they can relate to. Try, "This is sort of like having a fire extinguisher in the house—we may never use it, but it's smart to have just in case." Adolescents and teenagers can be filled in with slightly more detailed but still general statements, such as, "We've all been hearing a lot on the news about preparing for emergencies, and we think it's probably a good idea."

According to the CDC, you don't need to buy gas masks and hoard antibiotics in anticipation of a possible attack. If an emergency occurs, local and state health departments will inform you of the appropriate steps to take to stay safe.

To help families organize their efforts, the Red Cross now offers free preparedness courses. During these 1½-hour presentations, participants learn, among other things, basic first-aid techniques and how to create an emergency communications plan and evacuation plan. To find out if there's a course near you, call 202-303-4498 or visit www.redcross.org. If none are being offered in your area, ask for a free guidebook on preparing for emergencies and for specific ways to tailor your disaster supply kit to meet your family's needs.

Projecting a relaxed mood while talking to your child about emergency plans will go a long way toward reassuring her. "Children tend to accept whatever situation they find themselves in as long as the people they love and trust to take care of them seem calm and competent," says Penelope Leach, Ph.D., research psychologist in London and the bestselling author of *Your Baby & Child, Your Growing Child, Babyhood,* and *Children First.* Dr. Leach, who grew up in London during the bombings of World War II, recalls being more excited than scared about air raids and enemy planes. Other inconveniences simply seemed routine. "Having food shortages and blackouts after dark were just taken-for-granted parts of life," she says.

Keep in mind that what you're doing is beneficial for children. "Kids—and adults—are reassured by having an idea of what they'd do in an emergency," says Dr. Fassler. "A plan helps us manage and contain our anxiety." Of course, some children may be overwhelmed by all this information, particularly if it somehow triggers recollections of previous scary experiences. If you notice that's the case with your child, don't push it, says Dr. Fassler. Wait several days or weeks before bringing up the topic of safety measures again.

Above all, it's wise to place your efforts in perspective: "It's appropriate to reassure children that they're safe in their homes and in their schools," says Dr. Fassler, "because that's the reality."

6

Taking the Terror Out of Bioterrorism

—

Tackling the tough questions

—

By Jennifer Bush

As if discussing war and terrorism with children wasn't complicated enough, parents today have the additional burden of explaining concepts such as biological weapons, anthrax, and smallpox. For many mothers and fathers, the question becomes how to come across as calm when clarifying topics that send chills down their spines.

The truth is, regardless of how complex these ideas are, you can still be relatively straightforward when talking to your child about them, says Paul Ragan, M.D., associate professor of psychiatry at Vanderbilt University Medical Center in Nashville, Tennessee, who studied chemical and biological warfare as part of his Gulf War service. Children 5 and under will mostly want to know that they're safe and that their daily routine will remain unchanged, says Dr. Ragan. Preschoolers are unlikely to pose questions about chemical or biological weapons, and if they do, they're simply mimicking what they hear from adults, older siblings, or TV. He recommends avoiding details, which will only create confusion and anxiety at this age.

Kids 6 and older can grasp more detailed explanations, which include references to civic safety measures that protect schools, towns, and cities. But in general, experts say, the most effective and soothing way to talk to your child is with honesty—even if that means admitting you don't know the answer—and by keeping responses short and simple.

Here are some questions children 6 and older are likely to ask and the best ways to respond, from Dr. Ragan and Fred Henretig, M.D., a pediatric emergency room physician and toxicologist at the Children's Hospital of Philadelphia:

Q: What is anthrax?
A: It's a serious infection—like a bad cold or flu—that makes it hard for someone to breathe. But most people who get anthrax germs can take medicine so they don't become sick.

Q: What is smallpox?
A: It's a serious disease that starts as a cold or flu and then turns into a skin rash with blisters.

Q: What is bioterrorism or a biological weapon?
A: It's a way that people try to make someone sick by spreading germs.

Q: How can these germs spread?
A: They are released into the air and people breathe them in.

Q: How do I know that we're safe riding in trains or at an airport?

A: There are doctors, firefighters, and police officers who take care of this problem, and there are special soldiers who patrol the skies and streets to keep us safe.

Q: Can I get anthrax?

A: It's almost impossible. So far, only one child in the whole country has come down with anthrax, and he took medicine and was completely cured.

Q: Will Mom or Dad get it?

A: Only a few people in the United States have gotten sick from this problem, so it's very unlikely that we will get it. But if we did, doctors can help us just the same as they can help you.

Q: How would I know if I have anthrax?

A: You would become sicker than with a normal cold or flu—or you might get a bad rash—but we would be able to see that you weren't getting better the way you should. We would bring you to a doctor who would take care of you right away.

Q: Could we get smallpox?

A: Doctors tell us that no one has gotten smallpox in this country in more than 50 years, so it seems unlikely that anyone will get it.

Q: Am I safe?

A: Absolutely. You're just as safe as always.

Q: Does our country have biological and chemical weapons, and will we use them?

A: The government has some chemical weapons locked up in storage, but no one is planning to use them now.

If your child isn't asking questions about biological or chemical warfare and hasn't heard about the subject at school or home, there's no need to raise it with her, says Dr. Ragan. But if you know she's aware of it, it's better to broach the topic to limit free-floating anxiety and misconceptions. Discuss it with open-ended, exploratory questions, coaxing her to explain her thoughts in her own words. As always, give brief answers that stress solutions and security.

7

Teaching Tolerance

—

Helping children avoid prejudice in turbulent times

—

By Emily Fromm

Because of current events, your children may be exposed to racist comments or imagery, so it's vital that you provide an example of tolerance. *Child* spoke with Sheri R. Levy, Ph.D., who studies the development, maintenance, and reduction of prejudice among adults and children in the psychology department at the State University of New York at Stony Brook.

Q: Why is it important to talk with children about racism and prejudice at a time like this?
A: Prejudice among children can begin at a young age. By 4 or 5, most children can identify people's race or ethnicity. Between 7 and 10, they are beginning to develop sophisticated understandings of the similarities and differences among groups. Even though parents may not see or hear about racial conflicts and name-calling, it doesn't mean children are not exposed to—or participating in—

such acts. Also, while prejudice among young children tends not to be as hostile and intentionally hurtful as that of adolescents and adults, it's still harmful to everyone involved.

Q: Where do children pick up racist terms or ideas?
A: The media, parents, teachers, friends, and siblings can all influence children's attitudes. Children who have been exposed to the media's portrayal of recent world events may have formed negative associations about people who look Arab or have Arab-sounding names. These racist associations are what we most need to challenge among our children. Also, keep in mind that kids are quick to notice discrepancies between what we say and what we do. Be sure that your actions match your tolerant teachings; otherwise, children will follow your actions, not your words.

Q: What is the best way to handle it if your child makes a racist remark?
A: Racist statements among young children are most likely hollow and not meant to hurt another person. You should challenge negative remarks with positive ones. Around ages 7 to 9, children are able to understand the perspective of another person, so it's worthwhile to encourage them to consider how their remarks could hurt people.

Because some children may not be knowledgeable about other countries, this is an opportunity to teach kids about their rich cultures and religions. It's critical that children learn about not only our differences but also our similarities. So while you might point out differences in dress, food, or holidays, be sure to emphasize that people in other cultures share many of our interests: having fun, being kind, loving animals, spending time with family, and so on. Talking only about differences will fuel prejudice. Emphasizing the importance of getting to know people as individuals rather than members of particular groups will also help reduce intolerance.

Q: How can you answer a child who asks why some people hate America or would want to hurt Americans?

A: Children may ask such questions because they are worried about their own and their loved ones' safety. Start by reassuring them; then acknowledge that there is hatred in the world, but emphasize that there is also a lot of love.

Part Two

—

Learning From Others

—

For many of us, talking about war and terrorism is a relatively new concept; for others, it's been a reality for quite some time. In this section, you'll hear what's going on in our country's classrooms, where teachers are meeting the difficult responsibility of educating students about what's happening in the world in creative and inspiring ways. Next, you'll read the best advice from the accomplished members of *Child*'s advisory board, all of whom have dedicated their lives to ensuring the well-being of children. We also explore the methods used to reassure children in places where conflict is a way of life, such as Israel, Rwanda, and Uganda. In another chapter, leaders in the Christian, Jewish, Muslim, and Buddhist faiths offer their thoughts on how to discuss spirituality in these tumultuous times. Finally, we feature an essay by an American-born father living in Israel, who illustrates the importance of helping children feel secure when the world around them is wildly unstable.

8

Inside the Classroom

—

How teachers address war and terrorism

—

By Pamela Kruger

Even before the United States went to war against Iraq, first-graders at Agua Caliente Elementary School in Cathedral City, California, were talking about it. "Could Iraq's bombs get us?" one student asked his teacher, Pauline Gregg. Iraq has no nuclear weapons that can reach the U.S., she replied, pointing to a map.

The comments that twelfth-graders at Stafford High School in Falmouth, Virginia, made to government and global-issues teacher Sarah Roeske were just as tinged with anxiety. "Why does everyone hate us?" students asked.

For the first time since the Vietnam War, teachers have been struggling with how to talk about war, especially a controversial war that provokes strong opinions.

Perhaps because of the lingering trauma of the September 11 attacks, children of all ages have been peppering teachers with questions and showing signs of distress. Even those children who at home seemed unconcerned were asking questions in school, teachers say. "For months now, educators everywhere have been wondering, 'How do we teach this?'" says Charles Haynes of the Freedom Forum First Amendment Center in Arlington, Virginia.

Although curricula are created by state and local boards of education, teachers have great leeway in determining what they talk about in class and how they talk about it. And they take vastly different approaches, with some organizing daylong symposia for students on the history of Iraq and others virtually ignoring the subject. Although administrators' preferences and teachers' comfort with the subject certainly play a role in what is discussed, most teachers say they take their cues from students' emotional, as well as intellectual, needs.

In preschools, teachers tend to take the same tack as they did after September 11: They don't raise the subject or try to teach children about frightening current events. "My job is to reassure, listen, and distract," says Hanie Warshaw, a teacher at the Iris Family Preschool at Temple Sharey Tefilo-Israel in South Orange, New Jersey, a suburb of New York City. Since most parents try to shield preschoolers from news reports, she says the majority of children haven't discussed the war overtly in class.

Young children, however, don't always talk directly about their fears. Warshaw noticed, for instance, that one student seemed unusually anxious and had difficulty separating from his mother since the war began; even when he wasn't at school, he would tell his mom he felt scared in a particular building because "it isn't safe." Warshaw tried to reassure the boy by reminding him that his mommy would be back for him soon and that "all the adults are doing everything they can to take good care of you and help you have fun at school."

Elementary school teachers also see their job as offering reassurance, but how they accomplish that can differ dramatically. In November 2002, Gregg set up an e-mail relationship between her first-grade class and a U.S. Navy gunner's mate. Initially stationed in San Diego, the sailor moved with his ship to the Persian Gulf when the war started, and continued to e-mail the kids regularly.

The children asked about the size of the ship, whether he got to watch TV, and, of course, about war. Is he afraid? they wanted to know. (No, he wrote, he isn't.) Some kids also worried that he would be hurt. "I will not get hurt," he wrote, promising to have a pizza party with the class when he returned. Since the sailor was stationed on a ship at sea and U.S. ships were not being attacked, Gregg didn't feel the need to qualify his statement. "But if ships had started to come under fire, I would've discussed the possibility of the sailor being injured or killed," she says.

Isn't this too much information for 7-year-olds to handle? Gregg argues that many of her students already watch TV news— sometimes without the benefit of adults to help them understand what they see. "This is a chance for kids to have their questions answered, no matter what they are, from someone they trust in a comforting, nonthreatening way," she says. She hung a map on the wall, pointing out where Iraq and the U.S. are, because it reassures the children to see how far away the war is.

Children who were directly affected by September 11 require special attention. Many of the students in Pat Carney's fifth-grade class at New York's P.S. 34 were fleeing for their lives after the planes hit the World Trade Center. Their school—only three blocks away—was closed for several months afterward. As a result, when war became imminent, a consulting psychologist advised the teachers to invite children to air their feelings about the war, without letting war talk overtake the classroom. "What we learned from September 11 was that getting back to comfortable routines helps kids cope," says Carney.

So the day before the war started, Carney first asked her students to explain what they knew about the situation, then invited them to ask questions. She let them spout their opinions and corrected them when they got basic facts wrong, confusing Osama bin Laden, for instance, with Saddam Hussein. But instead of answering their questions—some of which she didn't feel qualified to answer—she tried to address their underlying concerns.

When a boy asked if this was the beginning of World War III, for example, she said, "It sounds like you're worried about how this will affect us here." While no one knows what will happen, she told him, after September 11, "the U.S. has a much better idea about how to be safe." As she explains, "My role as a teacher is to get the issue out there, correct misinformation, and make children feel personally safe, without promising that nothing will ever happen, because we don't know that."

While middle school teachers also try to ease students' fears, social studies teachers often use the war as a teachable moment, seeing it as a way to educate students about government and help them develop tools for analysis. At Millburn Middle School in Millburn, New Jersey, social studies teacher Timothy Corlett normally devotes one class a month to current events but decided to spend at least two classes a month solely on the war and gave his sixth-grade students special assignments, such as requiring them to read a weekly newsmagazine article about the war and write a paper summarizing the who-what-where-when-why of the story.

Like most suburban children, many of Corlett's students view war as a video game. "They'd say, 'Bomb Iraq!'" His hope is that they will not only develop the ability to read and analyze news articles but also begin to understand the realities of war.

At Liberty Hill Middle School in Killeen, Texas, a 15-minute drive from Fort Hood, a sprawling Army post, about half of the 906 students have at least one parent in the military. So while eighth-grade social studies teacher Michael Pearce spent time in the classroom explaining the U.N. resolutions and weapons inspections process, he chose not to stress the harshness of war.

A proud former Marine who was stationed in San Diego during the Gulf War, Pearce organized an assembly for the children whose parents were on active duty, inviting Fort Hood Army leaders to speak. "An army captain showed a video highlighting the U.S. military as the most technologically advanced army on the planet," Pearce says, "so kids know their parents are in good hands." Other army leaders stressed that their parents are heroes and gave each child a button saying so.

Pearce says no one objected to the politics of the presentation (though one military mom did say that all the talk about war upset her daughter). But frequently parents, politicians, and pundits do complain that politics creep into the classroom, especially in high schools, where teachers are more apt to discuss details of the war.

In 2002, conservatives such as Chester E. Finn, Jr., a former Reagan administration assistant education secretary who heads the Washington, DC-based education reform group The Thomas B. Fordham Foundation, released a scathing attack on the National Education Association and other school groups for developing September 11 curricula and lesson plans that emphasized, in the organization's words, "the dangerous idea of moral equivalence" and the "usual pap about diversity," instead of patriotism and civics.

And in 2003, parents in Maine's Army National Guard complained that some teachers were criticizing the war as "unethical," prompting the state's education commissioner, Duke Albanese, to issue an unusual rebuke, admonishing teachers to maintain neutrality in the classroom.

Many high school teachers say their role is not to reassure—that's the parents' job. Instead, they focus on trying to inform students, helping them appreciate the complexity of the issues. Roeske had her students debate the Iraq war and sometimes asked those with strong opinions to argue the opposite view. Caryn Stedman, a tenth-grade teacher at Metropolitan Learning Center in Bloomfield, Connecticut, organized a two-day symposium on Iraq for all the tenth-graders in her school before the war broke out. Then, with the help of a video communications company and ABC News (which later aired portions of the event), she arranged for 17 of her students to have a two-hour live video teleconference with Iraqi high school students. The kids talked about everything from the impending war to rap music. When an American student asked what the Iraqis would do if they could visit the U.S., for example, one Iraqi teen said he'd attend a concert by the rapper Dr. Dre. Stedman said this teleconference humanized the Iraqis, making her students more sympathetic to their plight.

Some high school teachers, like Roeske, studiously avoid expressing their opinions, not wanting to unduly influence students' views. But other educators feel differently, arguing that it's their basic right to express their views and that students are old enough to make up their own minds. In Madison, Wisconsin, high school teachers and students reportedly staged an anti-war protest in front of the school during their off-hours, while San Francisco's Board of Education adopted a resolution against the war.

Still, regardless of teachers' political views, they all seem to agree on one guideline: When talking to teens, be honest. "When my students say they don't understand how the U.S. went from hunting Osama to attacking Saddam, I say, 'I'm having a hard time understanding that too,'" Stedman says. "If you lie or try to hide your feelings, teenagers will know it and suspect you're hiding something even worse." And most important, when kids tell you that they're tired of talking about the war, pay attention. "Sometimes it gets to be too much for all of us," says Stedman.

 *9*

Words From the Wise

—

Child magazine's advisory board offers guidance

—

Compiled by Laura Gilbert

Just as every child is different, so is every family's perspective on what should be discussed in talks about war. Therefore, we asked our advisory board—a nationwide panel of leading authorities on children's advocacy, psychology, and development—what they most want parents to know about bringing up these potentially painful topics. Like virtually all the experts interviewed for this book, they agreed on the following principles: Be honest, answer simply, and don't make children feel any more scared than they may already be.

1. Follow Their Lead

"Let your child dictate the scope of the conversation. If you don't, you may bring up issues he isn't ready to handle. The last thing you want to do while you're answering questions is to introduce fears that weren't there before. So make an effort to answer the questions children have—not those you think they ought to have."

Will Wilkoff, M.D.,

pediatrician in Brunswick, Maine

2. Reassure Them

"Ultimately, whether you're explaining the history of a conflict or just the basics, children want to know that they're going to be safe. A good way to communicate this is to simply say, 'I'm here to keep you as safe as I possibly can.' They may ask if someone is going to hurt you or them with poison or guns or a bomb, and the best thing you can do is be honest. You can explain that in a war, people get hurt, but also reinforce that the soldiers are doing everything they can to make sure the war doesn't come to America. Explain the healing aspects of war missions too—that we're trying to bring food and medicine to people in areas where fighting is taking place."

Dorothy Singer, Ed.D.,
co-director of the Yale
University Family TV
Research and Consultation
Center in New Haven,
Connecticut

3. Turn Off the TV

"When a battle is replayed several times in a newscast, kids can't tell that it's just one battle. One finding after September 11 was that when TV stations would replay the footage, children thought dozens and dozens of airplanes were flying into buildings. I know that at first, I was drawn into all the war coverage and I wasn't paying attention to whether my children were watching or how they were responding to it. It finally hit me in the middle of the night that I needed to watch the news on my own time to find out what I wanted to know and not expose my children to it."

Barbara J. Howard, M.D.,
assistant professor of pediatrics
at the Johns Hopkins University
School of Medicine in Baltimore,
Maryland

4. Listen for Background Noise

"Even if you're monitoring TV exposure, there are subtle ways children take in information that we as adults don't notice as much. It's easy to turn on the car radio while you're driving a child to school. But then listen: It isn't just the words that are disconcerting. The background music, the tone, and the sound effects—repeated drumming sounds and explosions—can also be distressing for children. It even makes adults tense, but we barely notice; however, you have to peel away that layer and consider how the barrage of sounds can affect a young child."

Sara Wilford, *director of*
the Early Childhood Center
at Sarah Lawrence College
in Yonkers, New York

5. Consider Other Stresses

"Children already coping with loss and fear need special reassurance. Stress is cumulative, so children who have parents away from home, whose parents are divorcing, who are hospitalized, who have lost a loved one recently, or who in some other way are especially worried about issues of safety, stability, and security are at higher risk. Everyone connected with these at-risk children must make special efforts to offer physical, emotional, and intellectual nurturing and support."

James Garbarino, Ph.D.,
director of the Family Life
Development Center at
Cornell University in Ithaca,
New York

6. Know What's Normal

"Before you get upset about your child's response, consider that certain behaviors are appropriate at certain ages. Grade-schoolers, for example, may act out the aggression and violence of war and have play-fights where they vow to protect the family from the enemy. It's important for you to tell them that while they can have a pretend sword fight with a friend, they are not responsible for defending the family. If you explain that it's not their job, you may relieve them quite a bit. Grade-school children might get hung up on the details of death and want to ask gory questions. This is a natural response for kids this age and not a sign of anything more serious. Just answer their questions as calmly as you can.

"Adolescents, meanwhile, are egocentric, so they may take the war very personally. They may feel that they themselves could be the next victims or might have to fight, even if that's unlikely. At the same time, they're more apt to talk to their friends about their fears and not to their parents, so it can be frustrating to try to get through to them. Be on the lookout for additional risk-taking behaviors from older kids, because they may feel that since the end is near anyway, there's no reason to behave safely."

Barbara J. Howard, M.D.

7. Find Out What They're Feeling

"Children always feel that they are the cause of things. One way to get inside their heads is to explore through play what children are thinking and how they're processing information. Ask your child to show you what he thinks war looks like. Really take some time and get on the floor with him with puppets and toys. Have him create characters and let his thoughts unfold. Maybe the child can understand war only in terms of when he's gotten scrapes and had bandages put on them, or an older child might go overboard with shows of aggression. But by communicating on the child's level, you're allowing yourself to gain the information you need to handle the situation in the most appropriate way possible."

Sirgay Sanger, M.D.,
director of the Early Care Center
in New York City

8. Watch for Odd Illnesses

"Many times, if a child is under duress, there will be an increase in physical complaints that seem to have no logical explanation. A child's anxiety will often manifest itself in headaches, stomachaches, or sleeping problems. Yet if you ask, 'Is the war upsetting you?' the child might not be able to verbalize that as the root cause. Instead, ask the child to sit in your lap, and hold him very close. Ask if there's anything he would like to talk about. Sometimes, that intimacy and feeling of safety will be enough to help the child."

Will Wilkoff, M.D.

9. Address Violence

"When children ask why people do violent things, explain that all humans have the capacity for violence, and tie that to the anger a child sometimes feels and perhaps even acts on. Using her own experience as a basis, explain that the healthy way to deal with disagreements is always to talk about them, but sadly, sometimes the issue is so difficult that people fail to find a solution and decide to fight.

"In cases of war, we're generally dealing with two sides who have tried to talk, but that hasn't helped. Try to teach children to understand that both sides have reasons for their positions and get them used to looking at other people's opinions and trying to respect that they have a reason for defending their position. The best way to do this is by linking the point to a disagreement your child recently faced. This will help children understand not just that war isn't us vs. them but also why one child at school might report that her parents say war is wrong, even if you've told your child the opposite. Share your own feelings about the current war, but whatever these feelings are, stress that violence is something we should always try to prevent and that whenever we fail to find a peaceful solution it is a sad moment for all of us."

Roger Hart, Ph.D., *director of the Children's Environments Research Group in the psychology program of the Graduate School of the City University of New York in New York City*

10. Put It in Context

"Our goal shouldn't be to eliminate anxiety but to teach our children how to live with it and keep it in the background the way that children in other war-torn countries have been doing for decades. You can do this by letting your kids know you're there for them and giving some very concrete direction about what to do in case of an emergency. Of course a child is going to worry, and that's normal and appropriate. Our job is not to insulate our children but to help them develop the tools they need to grow up and become resilient adults. You don't want to underplay the seriousness of war, but at the same time, it shouldn't be a dominant theme."

Jerry Brodlie, Ph.D., *chief of the psychology department at Greenwich Hospital in Greenwich, Connecticut*

11. Maintain Rituals

"When the world seems so uncertain, children need to know that their daily lives will proceed in a relatively unchanged way.

Routines and schedules are important, and you don't want to make changes at a time when people are already anxious—it will only make everyone feel more so."

Sara Wilford

12. Encourage Emotions

"Urge your children to be creative through the use of blocks, papier mâché, clay, drawing material, paint—these things can help them express feelings that they may not be able to put into words. And work on artistic projects together to reaffirm that you're still a family unit. Take the trip to the zoo you've been putting off and slip a note into your child's lunchbox so he can see you expressing your love. You may even want to call your child a few extra times from work to let him know you're thinking of him."

Dorothy Singer, Ed.D.

13. Find Their Voices

"Even the most disenfranchised children, who live in countries where there have been wars and atrocities from the beginning, can come together when they learn their rights and begin to see that they have power. The tendency to view children as passive victims can sometimes be a disservice. Instead, you can empower your child to act on the issue. You might, for example, suggest that she write to the Red Cross or Save the Children to ask how she can contribute. This will help her realize she's a citizen and she can make a difference."

Roger Hart, Ph.D.

10

Lessons From Abroad

—

What we can learn from those who help children in war-torn countries

—

By Lisa Frydman

Afghanistan, Angola, Bosnia, Cambodia, Colombia, Iraq, Ireland, Israel, Rwanda, Sierra Leone, Uganda. Nations under siege, nations at war, nations divided. The list is long, the atrocities overwhelming. Bombs explode, guns are fired, parents are murdered, schools are shut down—but what happens to the children?

"Kids who are affected by war and terror sometimes lose faith in the ability of their parents and community to protect them and provide them with a safe and prosperous future," says Sara Cameron, communications officer at UNICEF in New York City. "In Colombia, for example, children who have been driven from their homes or who have witnessed acts of violence may see those who possess guns as possessing real power. One boy told me that he has to run home fast from school to avoid being recruited by one of the armed groups. He said that sometimes he has even stepped over dead bodies in the street."

Many children living amid armed conflict have nowhere to turn and subsequently fall through the cracks. International organizations are working to change things for these kids by creating programs and initiatives that harness the help of parents, peers, positive role models, and the community to form a network of support.

What most helps children who experience trauma is the presence of an adult who can reassure them that he will be there no matter what happens. "Children need this presence to be emotional," says Naomi Baum, Ph.D., director of Israel's National School Intervention Project for the Center of the Treatment of Psychotrauma in Jerusalem. "Parents are the most important people in determining how children react to trauma."

Guidance counselors, teachers, activists, and other professionals from all over the world agree that despite the worst-case scenarios, kids can bounce back. "Some children living in crisis are much more resilient than many adults, but only if they are given the appropriate attention, protection, support, and stimulation," says Marc Sommers, a research fellow with Boston University's African Studies Center and senior technical adviser for Youth at Risk for CARE USA. "In many areas of conflict, schools are among the first institutions attacked. Restarting schools in secure locations helps children, their parents, and their communities normalize their situations and support the long road from war to recovery. Classes must continue even if they're held in a basement." Indeed, in Bosnia, after years of war, the most repeated question orphaned refugee children would ask was: "So when does school start?" For children who've lost their families, their homes, and everything else connected to the past, school becomes a lifesaver—a way for a child to cling to something normal, the last remnant of what life was like before tragedy struck.

The clear message coming from abroad is that helping kids heal, especially those living in crisis situations, is a package deal. It involves combining the efforts of parents, relatives, peers, teachers, neighbors, and doctors to listen to what's on children's minds and allow them to express what's in their hearts. This is what we can learn from three especially troubled countries.

RWANDA: Understand, Listen, and Speak

The bottom line is kids need answers. Often parents don't want to tell the truth or speak their fears, but children as young as preschoolers see, smell, and feel the truth. "Kids pick up their parents' anxieties. It is crucial that this is acknowledged," says Marie Odile Godard, Ph.D., a psychologist based in Paris who has done extensive work in Rwanda. "Children must understand what we are going through and that it's tough even for us. I advise parents to listen to their children's fears and verbalize what they themselves feel. It gives children the sense that they're not alone. Expressing feelings is a key component for coping and healing for both adults and children."

Mike Wessells, Ph.D., psychosocial adviser for the Christian Children's Fund and professor of psychology at Randolph-Macon Woman's College in Ashland, Virginia, has worked in war zones around the world. He explains that how information is delivered has as much impact as the content. When dealing with a teenager who may ask tough questions ("What's the point of war? Why don't we just nuke those guys?"), Dr. Wessells emphasizes the importance of listening to the underlying concerns without trying to change the teenager's position. Instead, explore the complexities involved in any course of action.

ISRAEL: Camaraderie and Community

In a country threatened by constant terror attacks and suicide bombers, it's crucial that children feel a sense of control. "On one hand there is nothing we can do to prevent children from being victims of bombings, though we can avoid taking them to dangerous places or bringing them on buses, and instead drive them to school ourselves," says Danny Brom, Ph.D., director of the Israel Center for the Treatment of Psychotrauma affiliated with Sarah Herzog Hospital in Jerusalem. "But there is a way to help them feel less afraid. For young children, it's giving them the feeling that adults will protect them and tell them what to do and what not to do. For older kids, it's making them aware of signs of danger and alerting them to what they can do if they encounter trouble."

Projects to Help Children In *and* Out of War

Initiatives for helping children cope with war and terror are under way all over the world. Designed by organizations such as the International Rescue Committee, UNICEF, and the United Nations Educational, Scientific, and Cultural Organization (UNESCO), these out-of-the-box programs serve as inspiration for communities responding to kids in crisis. Here, a sampling:

Children's Involvement in the Truth and Reconciliation Commission, Sierra Leone

This project enables children to participate in Truth and Reconciliation hearings. It began in June 2001, when a group of war-affected children joined 40 national and international experts to develop recommendations for policies and guidelines on the involvement of children in the truth-and-reconciliation process, which is akin to a confession of atrocities committed during war. The workshop published its recommendations as well as the opinions of the child participants.

Peer-to-Peer Counseling, the Palestinian Territories

In this program, university students and other young volunteers are trained to provide psychosocial support, mentoring, and recreational activities for children and adolescents. Following the training, young volunteers conduct a series of school-based sessions with kids in the most violence-stricken areas. The project boosts self-esteem by providing a peaceful outlet for young people to express their views and deal with stress through positive activities such as a youth-to-youth hotline operated by university students. Parents are also involved in order to better support their children at home and in school.

War Boards, Israel

Designed to provide both visual and realistic answers to children about war, this project has been gaining momentum across the country. The idea is to hang a huge sheet of paper on the wall with sections for "Things we don't know yet," "Things we know partially," and "Things we know for sure." Parents and children fill in the information together as the war progresses. War boards help lower children's anxiety by sharing information and providing a truthful way to view the world around them.

Young Reporters Project, Albania

Troç ("straight talk") is a one-hour nationwide weekly television newsmagazine on social issues, produced entirely by young people ranging from 13 to 18 years of age. The idea is that kids become agents of change, informing the country about social problems and responsibility while learning reporting skills. The program has become a nationwide hit—it's now the country's top-ranking show.

Helping a Child in Crisis

Naomi Baum, Ph.D., director of Israel's National School Intervention Project for the Center of the Treatment of Psychotrauma in Jerusalem, suggests the following ways to ease suffering after a traumatic event:

- Speak to your child regarding the crisis and provide him with accurate information.

- Allow your child the room to express her thoughts without fear of being judged negatively.

- Reassure your child that you will continue to be there and that you will see him through the crisis.

- Keep in touch with your child's teacher to monitor her academic performance.

- Spend more one-on-one time with your child.

- Offer extra affection in the form of hugs and other physical contact.

Indeed, the biggest challenge in keeping kids safe may be in helping them acknowledge that the situation is dangerous and that it's natural to feel fear, says Dr. Brom. "It's better for kids to deal with reality than it is to avoid it." Beatrice Brom, a guidance counselor at a Jerusalem high school, says she encourages her students and her own children to trust their instincts. "If a child gets on a bus and feels something is wrong, my advice is to trust the feeling and get off. Knowing that they can actually do something helps empower kids."

Brom says teachers in Israel are encouraged to teach students the importance of community and camaraderie. The day after a suicide bombing, for example, Brom urges kids to get back into their routine but not ignore the tragedy: "Teachers are instructed to talk about the event during first period, because it's on everyone's mind. We're told to diagnose our students' level of involvement by raising questions like 'Where were you when you heard about the bombing?' and 'Do you know anybody who was involved?' "Next, teachers encourage coping by asking questions like "What can you do to feel better?" Ideas, such as helping each other, switching off the TV, and playing games, are collected in the class. Finally, instructors give accurate information about the event. The key, says Brom, is to model the combination of talking about the event when necessary and continuing the routine in a supportive environment.

Mooli Lahad, Ph.D., who heads the Community Stress Prevention Center at Tel Hai College in Kiryat Shemona, describes how some children in Israel play-act by recreating terror attacks—

imitating a terrorist carrying a bomb, the police, doctors, the dead, and the wounded. "As shocking as it seems, this is a child's way to learn about the situation and a natural way to cope through drama," says Dr. Lahad. "Though many parents don't like this type of play, it should not be discouraged."

In Israel the media's influence is strong, and the televised images of terror are gruesome. Dr. Lahad believes that parents should be with their children when they watch disturbing news. Research shows that a parental presence reduces the traumatic symptoms that otherwise may prevail when children watch horrific scenes. Talking about feelings and reality reassures children and provides the most important message of all: The parent is there for them, and together they'll get through the crisis.

UGANDA: Restoring an Identity

In Uganda, where thousands of children were abducted to serve as involuntary soldiers and, in the case of girls, as "wives" to some of the military officers, there is an abiding sense of hopelessness and powerlessness. But experts say it's helpful to acknowledge those emotions as a way to cope: "The expression of painful feelings during and after a war is crucial for giving children a sense of their past, present, and future," says pediatrician Lucia Castelli, M.D., program manager for the International Service Volunteers Association based in Uganda.

Creative methods (writing, talking, drawing, drama, music, and dance) are useful for helping children understand what happened to them. The goal is to restore a sense of identity and to build self-esteem. The focus, explains Dr. Castelli, is always twofold: the individual and society. If a child is made to feel important again, but her family and community do not accept her back, the wounds will reopen.

Many Ugandan teachers understand the importance of expression and have started to promote "peace clubs" in primary schools and "life clubs" in secondary schools as ways for children to freely articulate feelings at school and within the community at large, says Dr. Castelli. The main objective of forming groups and using creative activities is to help children and adolescents articulate their experiences. She warns educators not to push a child to talk about her trauma, however: "Willingness is crucial," she says. "The largest part of being empowered is giving the child the ability to make choices."

The vast majority of children living amid armed conflict cope reasonably well, despite the crises they see and experience, if they have at least one caring adult in their lives and some access to basic support structures—food, medical care, and protection, says Jane Lowicki, director of the children and adolescence project for the Women's Commission for Refugee Women and Children in New York City. "Kids learn not only to cope during conflict, but to become experts at surviving conflict through a process of rationalization, crying it out, fending for themselves, and caring for one another," she says.

The healing process is long, and the scars of war run deep, but it helps to keep in mind what a 15-year-old girl once told UNICEF's Sara Cameron: "Peace that begins in the heart of a child can cover the whole world."

 *11*

The Faith Factor

—

Religious leaders' best advice

—

By Lindsey Crittenden

In peaceful times, religiously minded parents can find it easy to present God and divine beings as sources of protection and love. But today, when children see increasingly violent images and hear news of destruction and harm at home and abroad, instilling faith in a benevolent power becomes more of a challenge—and an opportunity.

Turning to faith in times of conflict can help alleviate anxiety and helplessness. In March 2003, after the war in Iraq began, 52% of Americans prayed more than usual, a Gallup poll found. Religion helped 90% of adults cope after September 11, according to a 2001 study from the think tank RAND in Santa Monica, California. In this study, 35% of adults also reported that their child experienced symptoms of stress after the attacks. Children, who absorb our worldly worries, can also absorb the balm of belief. Here, six spiritual leaders share their thoughts on what matters now more than ever in talking to children about faith.

Reverend Lisa Hebacker, *Calvary Presbyterian Church, San Francisco: "Religion grounds all of us and so is especially important for children."*

- Try to model faith so that children will see it in you rather than have it forced on them. If you tell them, "Just put faith in God," they'll wonder what that means. But if you say that you feel God with you, and you hope they feel that too, they'll get the idea. Have your child envision that God is holding his hand.

- Prayer is an excellent way to convey the sense that God is with us and can hear our concerns. One 4-year-old in our children's chapel said, "I'm sad about the fighting on TV," so we prayed for God to be with the people getting hurt.

- I try to resist the urge to say everything will be okay, because we can't make that promise. But one promise we can make is that no matter what happens, God is with us. If I'm crying, God is crying with me.

- I would be very careful not to imply that God made the war to teach us a lesson. The war was our choice, not God's.

Father Dominic Grassi, *St. Josaphat Roman Catholic Church, Chicago: "Part of the faith experience is letting children know they are safe, they are loved, and that love is not going to be snatched away."*

- Christian faith tells us we are peacemakers. Children need to be told that good people differ and that we need to pray for those who hurt us—turn the other cheek, Jesus said. Of course, we have to protect ourselves when someone hurts us. But how we do it is important.

- We should be repeating that Jesus says to forgive people seven times 70 times. We can ask children to show on their fingers how many that is in order to make the point that this is hard to do but we still have to try.

- The prayer of St. Francis, which begins, "Lord, make me an instrument of your peace," is helpful. Sit down with children and read it, really take it apart. Jesus tells us constantly to love one another, to love our neighbor. Help children understand that the Iraqi children are our neighbors too.

- Do tangible things with children to show concern and increase empathy. Light a candle, ring a bell, say a prayer, draw a picture, write a letter to the President or to an Iraqi. Ask a child to think of a child his age in Iraq and pray for that child. Even if we don't know the child's name, God will hear our prayer. And we can thank God for our blessings by sharing our blessings.

Feeling Safe

Barbara Kohn, *Austin Zen Center, Austin, Texas:*
"Even when bad things are happening elsewhere, children can feel safe in the moment without ignoring the suffering of others."

- Buddhism teaches that life is filled with suffering and the way to end suffering is to avoid harming others, to be truthful, and to honor our involvement with others. Teach your child that he can reduce the world's suffering in his own way, by being kind and telling the truth.

- As master Thich Nhat Hanh says, "I am connected to all beings." So, to follow that logic, what happens to others in some ways happens to all of us. A child can understand that: Here I am, feeling sad, because someone is hurting. Tell children that that same connection also means we can take our love and send it to others through action.

- Talk to children about what it is to harm and what experiences they've had with differences and anger. Ask them, "What do we find in ourselves when we get riled up? Does it make life better for us? For others?" Ask, "What would Buddha do?"

- Help children to understand that what they are imagining is happening far away. I would ask, "Right now, in this living room, here with me, is there anything bad happening?" to help them to feel safe and to celebrate life in the moment.

Imam Al-Hajj Talib Abdur-Rashid, *Mosque of Islamic Brotherhood, New York City: "Children are familiar with conflict, and it's valuable to teach them to pray as a source of solace, a way to keep from being emotionally bombarded."*

- The religion of Islam encourages families to follow scripture and increase prayer, fast (for adults), and give to charity as a means of getting closer to God. We can help our children understand that we can maintain our faith in the face of tragedy and we can act in ways consistent with our beliefs.

- In the Koran, Allah tells us to "seek divine help with patient perseverance and prayer." In the Muslim faith, there is a special prayer, the *Du'atul-Qunoot,* that we recite in times of tragedy and crisis in addition to the five daily prayers. Young children are encouraged to pray at home and in the mosque.

- A child may ask, "Why does God let war happen?" I would answer, "God gives us the opportunity to act in a good or bad way and sometimes we choose the wrong way." Children can understand this. Take it into their own little world—two kids don't get along, so a teacher or parent acts as mediator. Explain to them that waging peace is long and difficult and takes patience and that we pray for it.

- When your children come to you disturbed, the first thing you should do is hug and kiss them so they'll feel safe.

Rabbi Susan Talve, *Central Reform Congregation, St. Louis: "I want kids to learn that God lives in every human being. I want kids to never give up hope."*

- Children as young as 3 can understand God as a loving force for good and can look to God to get through difficult times. We can help children do this through prayer and stories, through singing, through acts of loving kindness.

- Religious stories give children real examples of leaving oppression behind. In the Jewish tradition, the story of how Moses and Miriam danced at the shores of the sea after leaving Egypt tells children that redemption and liberation are possible. That helps to change our outlook so we can face challenges with a new perspective.

- If children ask about God's role in war and suffering, we can tell them that God is not to be confused with a superhero. We can help them understand that we are co-creators with God. Inside each of us there's a good inclination and a not-so-good inclination. Kids know that. We teach them to strengthen the good inclination. We can stop some bad things from happening, but not all bad things. In the physical world, things get broken.

- It's not helpful for children to demonize others. We can teach them that all people are created in the image of God. All creation is connected.

Reverend Thomas K. Tewell, *Fifth Avenue Presbyterian Church, New York City: "Spirituality can help children by showing how we go to God in troubled times."*

- When I talk to children about prayer, I tell them to talk to God as they talk to their best friend. Tell God all the good things and all the bad things. I also use stories of when God was with His people. The Bible gives the message that even if people fail, God can bring hope and new beginnings.

- Reassure children with your presence that you'll always be there: Read to them, give them a bath, dine together. After September 11, I told parents to spend more time with their children, to cancel optional commitments. Do not promise that you will always keep them safe because you don't know that you can, but assure them that you will try your best.

- If children ask why God allows war, tell them God gave human beings free will. You can say that in our freedom, we sometimes make mistakes. With younger kids, you can use the analogy of being told not to take a cookie before dinner but taking one anyway. You can say, "I could follow you around every second, but you'd never grow up."

- Kids can make a difference in the world; you can help instill compassion by saying, "Let's pray for the people who are fighting. Let's pray for both sides."

12

Safety Is a Frame of Mind

—

An essay

—

By Gershom Gorenberg

My son and I sit on the low stone wall in front of our Jerusalem apartment building, waiting for the school minibus. I sip my coffee; he tells me about the story he's been rereading, in which Hobbits and trolls battle, in the lovely passion of faraway, imagined danger. He's 12 and old enough to wait for the bus by himself, but we enjoy the few moments of quiet together before he goes to the noise of the classroom and I go to the office.

Then comes a boom: a raw, sharp blast that shakes my ribs, along with all the neighborhood's windows. My son pauses, then goes on about Hobbits. He has heard sonic booms before. I don't tell him what my journalist's ears know: This isn't the double ka-bang made by a plane and isn't followed by the roar of a jet. It is a bomb, so close that I can hear shrapnel falling.

The minibus pulls up. I shout, "Have a great day, kiddo," as he climbs in. When I come home, my wife has the radio on. A booby-trapped car had exploded in front of the mall three blocks away. Our pediatrician has her office in that mall; my wife had taken our 5-year-old there the afternoon before. Because the bomb went off before stores opened, no one was seriously injured. I drop onto the couch.

Don't misunderstand: I'm a satisfied product of the share-your-feelings era. It would have been natural to shout when I heard the explosion. I had to choose to postpone being afraid. If my son had asked what the noise was, I'd have said, "It could be a bomb, but we're okay. Let's hope everyone is." I'd have said it quietly and put my hand on his shoulder. Since he didn't ask me anything, I waited until I knew more. We live in an unsafe world. I'm particularly aware of that because for years my city has been in the midst of a violent upheaval. But no matter where we live, as parents, we all know of too many dangers that could harm our children. There are parts of town where we don't want our kids walking, times of night they shouldn't be out alone. We fear accidents and strangers and all kinds of things we see on the news.

We teach our kids about dangers that can be avoided, hoping that knowledge will make them competent to handle themselves—not terrified. We don't want their nights to be full of foreboding; we don't want everyone who looks different to be a bogeyman. We want our children to be safe and feel safe.

We need to remember that kids vibrate sympathetically with our feelings. When we laugh, they do too. Without even knowing why, they get angry when we do. You hold a child in your lap and talk softly to her before the nurse injects a needle because you know calm is contagious. So is fear.

In recent months, life in Jerusalem has felt nightmarish. I can tell my wife that feeling. I don't tell my children that I'm sometimes afraid for them, because I've realized that from me they need the only answers there are to a nightmare: a willing ear and a reassuring voice. My daughter has come home from kindergarten talking in quick, broken sentences about terrorists. I stroke her cheek and tell her yes, there are a few violent people out there, but most aren't like that—and someone isn't bad simply because he's different from us. I've explained to her older sister and brother, in the upper grades of elementary school, that we may need to skip a favorite hike this year. Being cautious, I said, is a way of being smart.

I talk about the news with them matter-of-factly, but we talk more about school, Harry Potter, and Hobbits. I have turned off TV reports about killings, as I would any show that's too gory. It's true that I can't turn off the world, but with the choice of my words and the tone of my voice, I can help my children feel safer and more cared for in it.

Part Three

—

Facing the Future

—

As we go to press with this book, there is no way of knowing
what lies ahead for our families, for our country, for the world.
What is certain is that children will be affected, some far more
than others. How can we help those who witness—or survive—
another terrorist attack or who lose a parent or loved one? In
an effort to address those questions, we present suggestions
from child development experts from all over the country. In
this last section, you'll find age-appropriate advice on ways to
recognize signs of distress and support children who are expe-
riencing it. You'll also learn how kids of all ages process death
and what you can do to help them cope. As a final word, we share
research on a subject that's relevant to all parents—what kind of
guidance children need in order to bounce back after enduring
trauma and loss.

13

When Children Feel Frightened

—

Words and actions to relieve their anxiety

—

By Sandra Y. Lee

No matter how hard you try to protect your children, you can't totally shield them from the outside world. They see graphic, scary images and hear talk about war and terrorist attacks on the domestic front. They also pick up on their parents' fears. "Taking in too much information from TV, hearing discussions among adults even if they don't quite understand what's being said, seeing people act differently, knowing people who are fighting overseas—these are all factors that are contributing to children's anxiety," says Sally P. Karioth, Ph.D., associate professor of nursing at Florida State University in Tallahassee.

Sometimes it may not be readily apparent that your child is feeling frightened and stressed. "Anxiety looks different in everybody," says Dr. Karioth, a grief, trauma, and stress expert who counseled survivors of the terrorist attack on the Pentagon as well as children who lost parents in the World Trade Center disaster. "Some people act agitated, others are more withdrawn." With kids, signs of stress can be subtle because they often don't say what they're feeling. As a result, parents have to be tuned in to their children's behavior. "Whether it's acting clingy, being disobedient, forgetting to do homework, or withdrawing, negative behavior is often a mask for a child's anxiety," says Laurentine Fromm, M.D., a Philadelphia-based child psychiatrist and president of the Regional Council of Child and Adolescent Psychiatry of Eastern Pennsylvania and Southern New Jersey.

What can you do to ease your children's fears? The first step is to make sure your family has an emergency plan. (See Part One, Chapter Five.) Taking concrete steps to protect your loved ones will make you feel better, and your kids will pick up on that. "Next, make sure you're in control of yourself and available emotionally for your child," says Victor G. Carrion, M.D., director of the Stanford Early Life Stress Research Program at Stanford University in Palo Alto, California. "If you're completely overwhelmed and need to express extreme anger or sadness, try to do it in private." (If the feeling persists and you feel depressed and helpless, consult a mental health professional.) Then, as you discuss the war and national security with your kids, remember to acknowledge your children's feelings and take your cues from how they're behaving and the questions they're asking. "And don't expect your child to be brave or tough," says Dr. Carrion.

The age-by-age advice that follows, courtesy of Dr. Fromm, with additional insights from Dr. Karioth and Dr. Carrion, offers more guidance about what to say and do. Keep in mind that children who have previously experienced trauma or loss may be at higher risk for feeling anxious and fearful. "The effect of stress on development is cumulative," notes Dr. Carrion. "New events can rekindle past experiences." If your kids still show signs of distress and you need more guidance, consult your family's pediatrician, a mental health professional, or a school counselor. In addition, don't hesitate to get help for yourself and ask family and friends to pitch in with your children if you're feeling overwhelmed. "There is no reason you should cope alone," says Dr. Fromm.

Ages 2 and Under

Signs of distress: Regressive behavior (such as wanting the bottle or pacifier after having outgrown it), clinginess, sleep problems, hitting, biting, frequent tantrums that are out of proportion to the cause, inability to be comforted

What to say: At this age, children are more inclined to be affected by your anxiety than to be frightened by events in the news. How will you know if your little one senses your stress? Instead of posing questions, she's more likely to *act* scared. In that case, you can say in a reassuring tone, "We love you very much and we're not leaving you. You're safe and we'll take good care of you." Going into any more detail than that may just frighten your child. On the other hand, if your child shows no sign of being anxious, there's no need to bring up the topic.

If your toddler is frightened by something specific—for example, he witnessed a caregiver crying because the news on TV reminded her of a relative who was fighting in the war—you can say, "I know Nanny was crying today. She was feeling sad, but I'm going to help her feel better. It's not something you did that made her sad." It's important to emphasize that last point because kids this age often assume they're responsible for the things that happen around them.

What to do: Most important, turn off the TV when your child is around. Young children are particularly sensitive to graphic images and may not understand that what's shown on TV involves events taking place far away or in the past.

In addition, children under 2 can't articulate what they're feeling. If your little one seems particularly upset, do some detective work to find out what may have happened that day to have caused it. Sit down and spend one-on-one time playing with your child. Check on her often, and provide lots of physical contact. The goal is to send the message that you are in charge and that your child's needs will be taken care of. Because young children are comforted by routines, try to keep to her normal schedule (mealtimes, bathtime with familiar toys, favorite bedtime stories). This may also not be the time to make a big change in her life, such as beginning toilet training or switching from a crib to a bed. If your toddler shows signs of distress, delay your plan for a few months.

If you have a childcare provider, make sure she follows your lead and ask her to keep you informed of your child's behavior. ("Please let me know if Max has trouble taking naps or if you notice any unusual or different behavior.") You might also say: "I know that times are scary and we're all on edge. If what's happening is getting in the way of caring for him, we can talk about it and come up with a plan so that all of us feel better." Finally, ask your caregiver to keep the TV and radio off and to stick with your child's daily routines.

Ages 3 to 5

Signs of distress: Clinginess, acting out, wanting to talk about the war and terrorist attacks all the time, stomach problems, sleep disturbances, regressive behavior (such as thumb-sucking and bedwetting), violent talk or play (such as repeatedly crashing toy airplanes together and pretending to blow things up)

What to say: Your preschooler may ask you questions about something he's seen on TV or heard from older children. If your child asks whether he's safe or if something like that can happen here, you can say, "I don't think anything bad is going to happen near our house, but if something does, we will keep you safe." The important thing is to answer the questions in a way that is meaningful to your child's world. Kids this age need to hear from you that you'll be there for them, and they need reassurance that they're in good hands. At the same time, they have an emerging sense of the larger world. They worry about how others are faring. So you might also tell your child, "Just like it's my job to take care of you, there are also a lot of grown-ups whose job it is to protect other people."

If your child seems anxious or is acting out, you can say, "I've noticed that you've been getting mad very easily. Is something making you angry or worried? If it is, we can talk about it." If she doesn't take the bait, let it go. Her mood may have nothing to do with the war; she may be upset about an argument she had with a playmate. But if the behavior continues, try again to determine what's bothering her.

What to do: In addition to verbal comfort, you can provide concrete assurances like using a night-light and leaving the door to his room open when it's time to sleep. Also keep the TV turned off when your child is within earshot. If you can't be with him, make sure he's with people who are very familiar to him. Kids this age also feel more secure with routines, so stick to his regular schedule as much as possible. Preschoolers, especially, may feel that they don't have as much control as they would like. One way to help them is to offer simple choices, such as "Which shirt would you like to wear—the green one or the blue?"

Make drawing materials, toy cars and trucks, and dolls or stuffed animals available to your child, and stay close as he plays with them. If your child draws a disturbing picture or uses the stuffed animals to act out something that's been upsetting him, you can say, "Can you tell me about what you drew?" or "Let's pretend—the Baby Bear doll is very scared, but Mother Bear doll will protect him."

If your child takes a step backward in her toilet training, be understanding and patient. It's not uncommon for children to react this way when they're feeling anxious or stressed. Most important, don't make her feel ashamed or embarrassed. In a calm, normal voice, you might say, "Oops, you had an accident. Let's clean it up together." If it occurs frequently, you can go back to diapers or training pants for a while until your child shows signs of being ready to try again.

Ages 6 to 12

Signs of distress: Headaches, stomachaches, sore throats, sleep problems, loss of appetite, intense fears about death, not wanting to leave the house or go to school, not wanting Mom or

Dad to go to work, new behavioral and learning problems at school, becoming the class clown or bully, getting into fights, feeling scared or angry, talking a lot about war and possible terrorist attacks

What to say: Kids in this age group can be very into war strategy and excited about the newest weapons. At the same time, they may be scared and angry. These conflicting emotions can be confusing for kids. You can help by telling your child: "It's okay to feel proud of what our soldiers are doing and to be scared of what's going to happen. People have many different feelings, sometimes at the same time."

It's also helpful for children this age to hear their parents reflecting out loud about their feelings: "It's so upsetting to hear about this in the news. It makes me sad." Hearing parents talk about their emotions helps school-age children sort out their own. The key, however, is to calmly comment on what you're thinking so your child will relate, rather than to use him as a sounding board for your own anxieties and worries. Remember, your job is to make your child feel better; it's not his to do the same for you. You can add, "If you have any questions about what's happening or what you're hearing, ask me and we can always talk about it."

You can also ask, "Did something happen today that seemed scary to you?" Then discuss her specific fears. For example, she may be worried about standing at the bus stop alone. She may be scared when she hears planes flying overhead. Or she may be worried about you taking an out-of-town business trip. You can be reassuring and truthful at the same time. You might say, "It's highly unlikely that anything will happen near us. And there are a lot of people in our government whose job it is to protect us." Find ways to comfort her, such as promising to call every night while you're out of town or arranging for a friend to wait at the bus stop with her.

What to do: If your child is still worried, give him something concrete to help him feel more secure, like a flashlight he can keep by his bed. You can get out a map or a globe and show him how far away the fighting is. In addition, try to be flexible. If your child seems to be dawdling and he needs more time to finish his homework, be patient. You can also invite your child to write about his feelings in a story that he can then share with you. Tell him, "I know there are things you may not know how to bring up, but here's a way you can put down what you're thinking." You should also limit TV. If you allow him to watch it, make sure you watch with him so you can discuss what you see. Even better, read a newspaper or magazine together—but screen the articles and photographs ahead of time so you can choose the least disturbing images and words.

Also make yourself available after school. For example, you can call your child at her after-school program just to check in and say hi. When you're home together, find activities you can do as a family: Work on a puzzle, build a birdfeeder, plant a garden, take walks after dinner. You can sign up for volunteer work or participate in a community activity like donating food and supplies to a relief organization. This is a good time to set aside evenings for playing board games, reading out loud, or watching nonviolent movies together. Finally, don't underestimate the power of family meals. Use that time to touch base with one another and talk about things that happened during the day.

Ages 13 to 18

Signs of distress: Withdrawing, irritability, argumentative behavior, sarcasm, headaches, stomachaches, an unusual number of worries about one's physical health, suddenly doing poorly at school, problems with peers

What to say: Angry actions, extreme indifference, or withdrawing may actually be a cover for feelings of anxiousness, hopelessness, and vulnerability. Instead of being direct and confrontational ("What's wrong with you?"), talk about your own feelings in a general way: "All this news makes a person worried about the future. It makes you wonder what's going to happen next." Teenagers have a sense of the larger context and are eager to participate in abstract discussions. By voicing your own feelings and worries, you encourage your child to talk about his emotions and help him make sense of his feelings. You can also let him know that these emotions take time to process—that you can't rush to feel better. Above all, make sure your child knows you're always available to discuss what's happening at school or in the news.

Continue to encourage discussion ("What do you think our government should do?") and really listen. If your child expresses a view that's contrary to your own, don't argue or try to dissuade her. Say, "That's interesting. What makes you think that?" This is an opportunity to learn what your teen is thinking, and kids this age really appreciate having their viewpoints heard. Without imposing your opinion, you can say, "Yes, some people think that and others think this."

You might also ask, "What's going on at your school? Are other kids upset? What are your teachers saying?" Discuss the school's safety plan and your family's plan of action in case of an emergency. If your teen plays it cool and doesn't seem all that worried, that's okay too. It's important to respect the fact that children have different ways of coping with a fearful, threatening situation.

What to do: Encourage your child to invite his friends over to your house and make them feel comfortable. This is another way of learning about his interests and concerns without being overly intrusive or obvious about it.

Keep in mind that although your teen may act grown up, she still needs the security and comfort of family. Now more than ever, stick with your family traditions and rituals; don't assume your child is too old for them. If your child is away at camp or in college, send care packages to let her know you're thinking of her. Your teen will also benefit from having adult role models she can turn to. Encourage your child to stay in touch with her grandparents, aunts, uncles, or other adults whom you respect and trust, such as coaches or teachers.

In the meantime, there are steps you can take together to combat feelings of hopelessness and powerlessness. You might volunteer with your child at your house of worship or a community service organization, send supplies to troops overseas, start a fund drive for relief organizations, or write letters to your members of Congress.

14

How Children of All Ages Handle Grief and Loss

—

The way kids feel—and what they need—when someone they love dies

—

By Jane Hammerslough

Whenever there's war and terrorism, there's death and grief. Helping a child who has lost a parent, relative, or close friend cope with his feelings of loss and mourning—which he may express in ways far different than adults do—will be a long-term process. It's important to encourage your child to ask questions and talk openly, says William M. Womack, M.D., associate professor of psychiatry and behavioral sciences at the University of Washington School of Medicine in Seattle.

In fact, one of the most beneficial things parents can do is share their own emotions with children old enough to understand what's going on, says Dr. Womack. But in doing so, be sure to address your child's main concern: that you'll still be able to help him manage his own sorrow. For children over 4, you can make this point by saying something like "I'm going to be here for you, but right now I need a little time to go through my sadness," suggests Dr. Womack. You might also relate your emotions to those your child has felt: "Remember how upset you were when you didn't get invited to Sam's party and you said you didn't want to talk about it and just wanted to be by yourself? That's kind of how I feel right now. But"— and this is key—"we can talk about it together later." Another helpful strategy is encouraging play therapy—in the form of storytelling, doll play, art projects, and more. This is a particularly useful way of expressing feelings that are otherwise hard for young children to identify and articulate.

How can you determine whether your child needs professional help to deal with her grief? Time will tell. After one to three months, your child's sadness should begin to lift. (This may happen more quickly in children under 6, says Dr. Womack.) But if your child doesn't want any part of her old routine, becomes irritable, or has trouble functioning at home or at school, talk to your pediatrician. The doctor can advise you on whether your child should be referred to a counselor, psychologist, or psychiatrist. If your child's grief is overwhelming—if she isn't sleeping well and has frequent nightmares, for instance—a doctor may prescribe medication. But that's the exception, says Dr. Womack: "For most children, it's enough to have a structured, supportive environment and an opportunity to talk."

What follows is a breakdown of how children process grief at each developmental stage, from Cathy A. Stauffer and Teri Busch, senior vice president and licensed clinical social worker, respectively, at Compassionate Care Hospice in Wilmington, Delaware:

How Children of All Ages Handle Grief and Loss

AGES	CONCEPT OF LOSS	GRIEF BEHAVIORS	WAYS TO HELP
Under 2	Little understanding of death	Separation anxiety, clinginess, crying	Lots of holding, hugging, and patience
2 to 6	Death seen as temporary or reversible	Sadness, aggression, regression, fear of going to sleep, nightmares	Play and art therapy, structured daily routine, giving children the words to help articulate their feelings
6 to 9	Gradual understanding of finality of death	Phobias, guilt, aggression, sleep problems	Art therapy, regular routines, reassurance
9 to 12	Awareness of finality of death, but difficulty conceiving the death of a loved one	Anger and defiance; phobias; guilt; aggression; possessiveness; sleep problems; changes in grades, attitudes, friends	Therapy using art, plays, skits, journal writing, letters, other ways to connect to memory of loved one; honesty and openness
12 and up	Understanding that death is universal, final, and inevitable; little sense of own mortality	Risk-taking; anger; defiance; changes in work habits, grades, attitudes, friends	Peer-group therapy, parents setting limits and offering opportunities for communication

15

Six Keys to Boosting Your Child's Resilience

—

What really helps kids triumph over adversity

—

By Tracy Perez

Experiencing loss as a result of war or terrorist attacks is a fact of life for many children. Fortunately, research on the adjustment of children who have felt the effects of horrific life events shows that with time and the proper support system, many of them can overcome the odds and go on to lead happy and successful lives.

The ability of children to persevere under even the harshest conditions is perhaps best reflected in a study of Cambodian youth led by a team of prominent psychologists in the field of resilience. Researchers from the University of Minnesota in Minneapolis followed young Cambodians who survived the massive trauma of war in their country in the 1970s and later immigrated to Minnesota. While many of the young people suffered symptoms associated with post-traumatic stress disorder, many were getting on with their lives as adolescents in a new country. They performed well in school, made new friends, and became productive citizens in the United States.

"It all comes down to whether children feel safe in their world," says Betsy McAlister Groves, a licensed social worker, author of *Children Who See Too Much*, and founder of the Child Witness to Violence Project at Boston Medical Center, an organization dedicated to helping children who see violence firsthand in their homes and communities. "The safer kids feel, the better they'll be able to bounce back after a tragic event."

While certain similarities exist among resilient children, Groves emphasizes that the ability of any child to overcome a tragic loss greatly depends on how closely it affects her. The coping process of a child who has lost a parent or sibling as a result of war or terrorism will be far more complex than that of a child facing the death of a neighbor or acquaintance.

Groves, along with other experts in the field of resilience research, has identified some key similarities that help kids feel secure—and therefore better able to cope with tragic events. Here, the six factors at the top of their list.

1. The presence of a positive adult Children with a supportive figure in their lives—whether a parent, relative, teacher, or coach—show a much greater ability to cope with a tragic life event, says Groves: "Children are hopeful when they have someone they can discuss their fears with who believes in them."

The link between the presence of a supportive adult in a child's life and his ability to remain resilient was first examined in a groundbreaking study performed by Emmy Werner, Ph.D., research professor of human development at the University of

California at Davis. Dr. Werner studied the lives of disadvantaged children living on the island of Kauai in Hawaii for almost two decades. Through her research, she found that all the high-resilience children involved in the study had at least one caring and supportive adult, either a family member or a teacher. According to Dr. Werner, the adults listened to the children, challenged them, and rooted for them. Many of these kids went on to have successful lives with healthy social relationships and stable careers.

2. Good problem-solving skills Resilient children seem to possess similar internal qualities, like the ability to work through problems. Groves recalls a child she worked with who was afraid to walk to school because he lived in a violent area. One day, he noticed a police officer standing nearby. From that day on, he decided to make eye contact with the officer every day on his way to school. By doing this, Groves says, he found his own way to feel safe.

3. A strong set of values Sharing your personal beliefs and values with children bolsters their resilience in a number of ways, according to Richard Gallagher, Ph.D., psychologist and director of the Parenting Institute at the New York University Child Study Center in New York City. "Instilling children with powerful beliefs helps them look to the future, feel connected to a larger social group, and engage in more positive behavior," says Dr. Gallagher. "In fact, even children who share the values of groups that endorse violence have better adjustment than children who have no values at all."

4. An understanding of the actual probability of tragedy and disaster Children have a tendency to personalize negative events and believe they could easily happen to them or members of their family, says Dr. Gallagher. It's important for adults to help children recognize that tragic events such as terrorist attacks are very unlikely to affect them or members of their family. Use the events of September 11 as an example. Explain that despite the great loss of life on that day, an overwhelming majority of people were not physically harmed. Most people who were traveling on airplanes at the time of the attacks returned to the ground safely, and only a few buildings in a few areas in the country were physically affected. "A realistic outlook should help free children from constant worries that they will be harmed," Dr. Gallagher says.

Of course, some children are more prone to worrying than others, so it's important for parents to look for signs that indicate the need for professional help. A child who is unable to focus on everyday tasks and seems unduly preoccupied with talk of war or violence may need to see a mental health specialist. If you notice these behaviors in your child or if she complains of headaches, stomachaches, or other stress-related illnesses following a tragic event, consult your pediatrician.

5. Predictability Don't underestimate the importance of keeping a sense of routine in your child's day-to-day activities as a way to help him maintain a positive outlook on life. Previously scheduled events like birthday parties or family gatherings should not be canceled because of what may be going on in the rest of the world, Groves says: "In uncertain times, sticking to a normal routine may be one of the most comforting things you can do for kids."

6. A sense of control Children remain hopeful when they can actively contribute toward building a better future. Adults can help children feel they're making a difference by asking them if they'd like to commemorate a loss by sending cards to victims' families or by donating their time to helping victims of violence. "Children who believe that they can take steps to make their future better and who believe that adults are working to create a better world have better mental health," says Dr. Gallagher, "even when they experience years of traumatic events."

Where to Turn
for More Information

—

Resources

—

In reporting and writing this book, we asked our experts for resources they considered especially useful. Refer to them for further help in talking to your children about war and terrorism.

U.S. Organizations

American Academy of Child and Adolescent Psychiatry
Phone: 202-966-7300
Web site: www.aacap.org

American Academy of Pediatrics
Phone: 847-434-4000
Web site: www.aap.org

American Psychiatric Association
Phone: 703-907-7300
Web site: www.psych.org

American Red Cross
Phone: 202-303-4498
Web site: www.redcross.org

Centers for Disease Control and Prevention
Phone: 800-311-3435
Web site: www.cdc.gov

Federal Emergency Management Agency
Phone: 202-566-1600
Web site: www.fema.gov

Military Family Resource Center
Phone: 703-602-4964
Web site: http://mfrc.calib.com

National Alliance for the Mentally Ill
Phone: 800-950-NAMI
Web site: www.nami.org

National Association for the Education of Young Children
Phone: 800-424-2460
Web site: www.naeyc.org

Save the Children
Phone: 800-SAVETHECHILDREN
Web site: www.savethechildren.org

Canadian Organizations

The British Columbia Teachers' Foundation
Phone: 604-871-2283
Web site: www.bctf.bc.ca

Canadian Pediatric Society
Phone: 613-526-9397
Web site: www.caringforkids.cps.ca/behaviour/Terrorism.htm

United Nations Association of Canada
Phone: 613-232-5751
Web site: www.unac.org

War Child Canada
Phone: 416-971-7474
Web site: www.warchild.ca

Books and Guides

Coping with the Stress of Terrorism and Armed Conflict, available at
www.hc-sc.gc.ca/pphb-dgspsp/publicat/oes-bsu-02/index.html

The Emotional Cycle of Deployment: A Military Family Perspective,
available at www.hooah4health.com/environment/deployment/
emotionalcycle.htm

Guidelines for Helping Children During War, by Diane Levin, Ph.D.,
available at www.truceteachers.org/war.html

The Help Guide to Guard & Reserve Family Readiness, available at http://www.defenselink.mil/ra/family/toolkit/pdf/helpguide.pdf

Let's Talk About Living in a World With Violence: An Activity Book for School-Age Children, by James Garbarino, Ph.D., available at bookstores

Index

A
Age-specific recommendations.
See also Grade-schoolers;
Preschoolers; Teenagers
death/grieving, 99
military duty explanations, 23–26,
28
stress management, 89–96
world events discussions, 5–7,
19–20
Anthrax, 38, 39
Anti-Americanism, 15, 43, 47
Anxiety. *See* Fear; Stress

B
Bad people, 8–9
Behavior
good vs. bad and, 8–9, 15, 75, 78
normal, knowing, 58–59
unacceptable, 8
Bioterrorism, 37–40

C
Chemical weapons, 40
Counseling, 27, 88, 89, 98, 104

D
Death, 97–99
Disaster supply kit, 33–34

E
Emergency plans, 31–36, 88
children involvement, 31–32, 34–
36
communications plan, 32–33
disaster supply kit, 33–34
preparedness courses, 35
Red Cross/FEMA
recommendations, 32–34

Emotions
encouraging, 62
sharing, 97–98
Empowering children, 62

F
Faith, 73–80. *See also* Prayer
alleviating stress, 73
Buddhist perspective, 76
Israeli essay, 81–83
Jewish perspective, 78–79
Muslim perspective, 77–78
Presbyterian perspective, 74, 79–80
Roman Catholic perspective, 75
Family stories, 17–22
Fear, 87–96. *See also* Stress
age-specific recommendations,
89–96
parents revealing, 9–10, 25
terrorism and, 9–10

G
Good vs. bad, 8–9, 15, 75, 78
Grade-schoolers
bioterrorism and, 37–40
classroom discussions, 49–50
death/grieving and, 97–99
explaining military duty to, 21–22,
25, 28–29
explaining war to, 17–22
managing stress, 92–95
normal behavior, 58
world events discussions and, 6, 7
Grieving, 97–99

I
Illnesses, 59–60, 91, 92, 95, 104
International lessons. *See* War-torn
countries

M

Military duty, 20–22, 23–29
  classroom discussions, 51–52
  explaining, age-specific tips, 23–26, 28
  parent stress and, 26–27
  single parents and, 27
  TV reports and, 25, 26, 89

P

Peer-to-Peer Counseling, 67
Playing, as diversion, 18, 27, 28
Prayer. *See also* Faith
  advice, 74, 75, 77, 78, 79, 80
  for military, 18, 20
  terrorism increasing, 73
Prejudice, 41–43
Preschoolers
  classroom discussions, 48–49
  death/grieving and, 97–99
  explaining military duty to, 24–25
  explaining war to, 17–22
  managing stress, 89–92
  world events discussions and, 5–6
Professional help, 27, 88, 89, 98, 104
Protests, 14

Q

Questions
  following child lead, 55
  not knowing answers, 10
  types asked, 4

R

Racism, 41–43
Reassuring stories, 17–22
Red Cross
  preparedness courses, 35
  safety measures, 32–34

Religion. *See* Faith
Resilience, boosting, 101–105
Resources, 107–110
Routines, 61–62

S

School discussions, 47–53
  grade school discussions, 49–50
  preschool discussions, 48–49
  teenagers, 50–53
School emergency plans, 33
September 11, 2001, ix
  children directly affected by, 49–50
  classroom discussions, 49–50
  curricula, 52
  faith and, 73
  increasing prayer, 73
  replaying, 20–21
  stress and, 31, 47
  explaining military duty to, 24–25
  as tragedy explanation example, 104
  TV reports and, 56
Single parents, 27
Smallpox, 38, 39
Stress. *See also* Fear
  actions relieving, 90, 91–92, 94–95, 96
  age-specific recommendations, 89–96
  alertness to, 29
  boosting resilience, 101–105
  children, 24, 25–26, 31–32
  cumulative effects, 31–32, 57–58
  encouraging emotions and, 62
  faith and. *See* Faith
  grieving and, 97–99
  identifying, 59–60, 87–88, 89, 91, 92–93, 95